Don't be a victim of the fine print!

- • Should you modify life insurance after age 65?
- • Can you depend on your insurance for retirement income?
- • Does a hefty savings account cancel the need for life insurance?

Life insurance should be protection. This guide will help you decide what's best for your family's needs, and how to avoid being swamped by confusing terms and jargon.

THE CONSUMER'S GUIDE
TO LIFE INSURANCE

J. Tracy Oehlbeck

PYRAMID BOOKS NEW YORK

THE CONSUMER'S GUIDE TO LIFE INSURANCE

A PYRAMID BOOK

Copyright © 1975 by Tracy Oehlbeck

Pyramid edition published May 1975
Third printing, July 1976

Library of Congress Catalog Card Number: 75-4073

Printed in the United States of America

Pyramid Books are published by Pyramid Publications (Harcourt Brace Jovanovich, Inc.). Its trademarks, consisting of the word "Pyramid" and the portrayal of a pyramid, are registered in the United States Patent Office.

PYRAMID PUBLICATIONS
(Harcourt Brace Jovanovich, Inc.)
757 Third Avenue, New York, N.Y. 10017

TO LOUISE

CONTENTS

FOREWORD

This effort is respectfully dedicated to the widows and orphans of the future, the beneficiaries of most life insurance policies. Unfortunately, it's too late for many of the *present* widows and orphans who are now suffering the consequences of greedy and self-serving techniques of the life insurance industry—an industry that loudly proclaims its own greatness, but which has failed miserably in protecting our families.

In 1969, a survey of widows was made by the Life Insurance Agency Management Association and the Life Underwriter Training Council to find out how well the life insurance industry was doing its job. The women who were interviewed were all widows of men who were less than sixty-five years of age at time of death—men still in their earning years—not senior citizens. Here are some gems from *The Widows Study*:

GEM #1: Fifty-two percent of the widows received less than $5,000 in life insurance proceeds. This is less than six months' income for the average family.

GEM #2: Fewer than one of eight home mortgages was covered by life insurance. Mortgage insurance is dirt-cheap, but most widows inherited a debt instead of a paid-for home.

GEM #3: Only forty-three percent of the widows were contacted by a life insurance agent following their husband's death. This poor servicing of death claims is partially explained by the high turnover of life insurance salesmen, but it seems that the home offices that paid the claims could have arranged for someone to assist these women. The life insurance industry calls itself a "service" industry, does it not?

GEM #4: In many cases, the insurance money received

by the widow was less than the final expenses connected with her husband's death. Fifty-eight percent of the widows stated that medical costs alone amounted to $2,000 or more.

GEM #5: After paying average final expenses of $3,900 (medical, funeral and miscellaneous bills), the average widow ended up with about $8,000 in cash. How long could *your* widow maintain your present standard of living on $8,000?

To date, *The Widow's Study* has been circulated mainly within the life insurance industry only. It is making waves and the companies are justifiably worried about their public image. Can you imagine how worried they would be if *The Widows Study* were to be headlined in the newspapers *a la* Watergate? Or discussed by columnists and television commentators?

Another set of grim facts was uncovered in a survey by Anchor National Financial Services, Inc. (ANFS), a financial planning services company headquartered in Phoenix, Ariz. These are the results:

Horror Tale #1: Within 18 months, 52 percent of all widows have dissipated the insurance benefits of their husbands; within 60 days one out of four widows has exhausted *all* her insurance money.

Horror Tale #2: The average of all death benefits left to a widow today is only $12,000—including insurance, Social Security, V A benefits, pensions, etc.—against which the average cost of death expenses, including hospitals, doctors, funeral, etc. is $4,000. And if you exclude accidental death and use only medical death, that average cost goes up to about $8,000.

Horror Tale #3: Out of every four widows, one is under age 45 with children and the average span a widow spends raising children is six years.

Horror Tale #4: Social Security checks take an average of four months before they arrive after death.

The Institute of Life Insurance is the public relations organization of the life insurance industry and publishes the *Life Insurance Fact Book* each year. This publication is largely self-praise of the life insurance industry. Here are some items from the 1973 edition, with the self-praise deleted:

ITEM #1:

1972 Investment Income	$12.127 Billion
1972 Death Benefits Paid	− 8.007 Billion
Excess Investment Income	$ 4.120 Billion
1972 Life Insurance Premium Income	$24.678 Billion

Plainly enough, the life insurance industry had more than four billion dollars left over from its investment income after paying death claims and could use the 24.678 billion dollars of life insurance premiums however it pleased.

This 24.678 billion dollars was life insurance premium income only and did not include:

1972 Annuity Premium Income	$ 5.503 Billion
1972 Health Insurance Premium Income	$14.318 Billion
1972 "Other" Income	$ 2.222 Billion

This all adds up to 58.848 billion dollars of income for just one year! What amount do you suppose went for plush offices, juicy commissions, conventions for salesmen and similar expenditures that didn't benefit you, the premium payer, whose money is being used? Remember, out of this 58.848 billion dollars, only 8.007 billion were paid in death benefits.

ITEM #2: The average death claim paid in 1972 was $2,774. This was an increase of $89 over the 1971 average of $2,685. A man *could have had* more than one policy, but you will probably agree that these figures are rather dismal nonetheless.

ITEM #3: At the end of 1972, total assets of the life insurance industry were 239.73 billion dollars, an increase of 17.268 billion dollars from the year before. This tremendous pool of insurance buyers' money could have helped many families finance a home through FHA and VA mortgages.* However, the number of nonfarm FHA and nonfarm VA mortgages owned by U.S. life insurance

*Home loan plans subsidized by the Federal Housing Authority and the Veterans Administration.

companies has steadily declined since 1966. The reason? More lucrative investments were available elsewhere. And this is the industry that says it contributes so much to so many!

ITEM #4: The life insurance coverage of the average family in 1972 was $22,900, which is roughly equivalent to two years' income. (The 1972 average family income was $11,200.) When you subtract the normal medical, legal, burial, and other final expenses, the remainder is substantially less than two years' income.

ITEM #5: The average American family pays about $250 per year for personal life insurance coverage of around $12,000. (Group life insurance is not included in these figures.) On a per-thousand basis, this figures out to $20.83 per $1,000. In comparison, a thirty-five-year-old husband and father can buy decreasing term to age 65 for $3.92 per $1,000 or five-year renewable and convertible term for $3.09 per $1,000. In amount of protection, the average family cost of $250 per year would buy these amounts of coverage:

$77,000 of five-year renewable and convertible term

$61,000 of decreasing term to age sixty-five

Compare these amounts with the average $12,000 of family protection, and it is quite obvious that most families are not getting full value for their life insurance premiums.

NOTE: About sixty percent of death benefits paid result from the death of men under age sixty-five.

At this point I wish to make it clear that I am not against the idea of life insurance. It is a very essential part of a family's financial planning. I also believe that the life insurance industry is a necessary industry, and I am not advocating that its function be taken over by any form of federal or state bureaucracy. What I do oppose—and very strongly—is the way that life insurance is too frequently presented and sold. The promise to the buyer of "getting something back" results in an overcharge to the *buyer* and a serious disservice to the *consumer*.

When we speak of the consumer, we usually refer to the buyer of a product or service. However, in the case of life insurance, the buyer is usually not the consumer. The consumer is the beneficiary of the life insurance policy. When a husband and father buys insurance on his life, his purpose is to provide money for his survivors when he dies. Therefore, the consumers are the widows and orphaned children left behind.

Many corporations and partnerships are also sold life insurance on the basis of "getting something back" and consequently pay more than is necessary for protection against the premature death of key personnel. In most of these cases, the beneficiaries are the companies or partners, not the widows and orphans. While I see no good reason for a smart businessman to overpay for life insurance, this is not my immediate concern. I am much more concerned about how overpriced life insurance damages the financial security of widows and orphans.

Life insurance is often presented as a savings or investment program. In my opinion, this is the worst possible method of saving money for future needs such as retirement, children's education, a trip around the world, or some other financial objective. There are many better ways of accumulating money than by giving it to a life insurance company to save for you. This matter will be discussed, but the idea of "Buy Term and Invest the Difference" is not the main theme of this book.

Emphasis will be on the benefits of pure protection term life insurance for family protection—the primary reason for life insurance. The various forms of life insurance will be discussed and (hopefully) will make this important subject more understandable.

So that you will have a better idea of what to look for and to make intelligent and informed decisions—STUDY WELL! You may prevent your wife from being one of the miserable statistics of a future *Widows Study*.

Sincerely,
J. Tracy Oehlbeck
Dayton, Ohio

CHAPTER ONE

WHAT IS LIFE INSURANCE?

What is life insurance? This may sound like a rather ridiculous question because everyone knows what life insurance is. Or do they? Judging from the statistics of *The Widows' Study,* a high percentage of their husbands weren't too well advised or informed of what life insurance was all about. The figures from the *Life Insurance Fact Book* aren't exactly encouraging either.

Life insurance is protection against the premature death (often sudden and unexpected) of a person who is responsible for the financial security of others. A husband and father is responsible for his family's food, clothing, shelter, education and other living expenses. He is obligated to try to earn the money needed to pay these bills. If he dies before his obligations are taken care of, the money that he didn't live long enough to earn must come from some other source. *Life insurance is therefore a substitute for money.* If a husband and father doesn't have enough money to cover his obligations in case of his death, his family suffers the consequences.

If you are the average husband and father, you probably have a mortgage on your home. Whether you realize it or not, you have another—and much larger—mortgage to be concerned about. This is the amount of money your family will need if you are no longer around to provide it.

For example, let's say you are age 35, your wife is age 30, you have two children ages 5 and 7 and a $25,000 mortgage on your home. If you were to die tomorrow, your survivors' financial position would look something like this:

Requirement	Amount
Home mortgage	$ 25,000
Two college educations @ $15,000 each	30,000
Income of $100 per month for 15 years until older child reaches age 22	18,000
Income of $100 per month for 17 years until younger child reaches age 22	20,400
Income of $300 per month for 17 years for your widow from age 43 to age 60	61,200
Final expenses	3,000
Reserve fund	5,000
Grand total	$162,600

Did you realize that you had a hidden mortgage of $137,600 in addition to your home mortgage of $25,000?

NOTE: Social Security (assuming that you are covered) would provide a basic (but usually inadequate) income for your survivors. The wife receives Social Security as long as there is one child under age 18. The above figures are in addition to Social Security payments and are not inflated. Don't conclude that your widow and orphans would be lolling in luxury.

Your total obligations (mortgage) decrease with time. Each payment on your home mortgage reduces the loan balance. Each dollar that you salt away for your children's education reduces this obligation. Each paycheck that you bring home reduces the number of weeks that they would be dependent upon life insurance proceeds.

When your home is paid for, when your children are through college and on their own, when you have accumulated money in savings accounts, stocks, bonds, mutual funds, pension plans and other investments, you will need much less life insurance than at present.

Obviously, you will not accomplish these objectives overnight unless your rich uncle remembers you in his will. In most cases, your main concern is *time*. You need *time* to pay off your mortgage. You need *time* to earn the money to feed and clothe your family. You need *time* to accumulate the money for college. If you die before these obligations are completed, the *time* that you were not granted must be compensated for in some other way. This is a second definition of life insurance. It is *time* that you might not have to complete your financial obligations.

To summarize, life insurance is *money;* life insurance is *time;* it is a safeguard against insufficient money and insufficient time. This may be all boiled down to one word— PROTECTION.

Now let's see how you can obtain this protection without bankrupting your budget.

CHAPTER TWO

INSURANCE JARGON

At times it seems that the basic philosophy of the life insurance companies is: "If you can't sell 'em, confuse 'em." Words and phrases such as cash value increases, fifth dividend option, paid-up additions, net cost, interest-adjusted method, nonforfeiture values, etc. are standard insurance jargon. They are meaningful to the companies and salesmen, but are often only partially understood by the buyer.

Too often, this insurance double talk produces only one result: confusion. When the salesman whips out the multicolumned, computer-prepared illustration of his splendiferous plan, the poor client is completely befuddled. Rather than admit his lack of understanding, he nods his head, looks intelligent and signs the application just as though he were aware of what he is getting. Most of the time he doesn't know if he is being sold whole life, twenty-payment life, twenty-year endowment, or even what the differences are.

Life insurance doesn't need to be perplexing. So let's try to remove some of the cloud cover and make this important subject more understandable.

In spite of the multitude of names and titles generated by the life insurance companies, there are only two forms of life insurance:

1. Term insurance—with no embellishments.
2. Term insurance combined with some sort of savings element, such as cash value and/or dividends.

NOTE: As you can see, term insurance is present in both forms of life insurance.

Term insurance is protection against loss of life during a specified period of time. In this respect, it is similar to the fire insurance coverage you have on your home. This protects you against loss from fire and pays off only if you have a claim while the policy is in force. It's pure protection.

NOTE: "Term" is also a four-letter word to many companies and salesmen because it means lower income and commissions.

The combination of term insurance and a savings element (cash value and possibly dividends) is lovingly referred to as "permanent" insurance by its advocates. By selecting this nice, solid-sounding title, they imply that term insurance by itself is therefore "temporary" insurance and that "permanent" insurance is the only type that you should buy.

NOTE: You can buy term insurance that stays in force to age 100. Would you consider this "temporary"?

The life insurance industry dearly loves to sell permanent insurance because the premium per $1,000 of death benefit is substantially higher than for pure protection term insurance. The higher premium produces more income for the company and larger commissions for the salesman, but lower protection per premium dollar for the buyer.

To help you understand how this wonderful permanent insurance works, study this diagram:

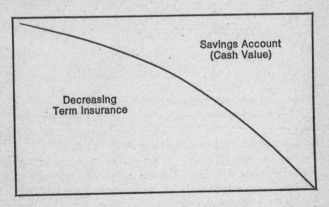

Typical Permanent Insurance Policy

Let's say this is a $1,000 policy and therefore would have a face value of $1,000 in case of your death. After several years of premiums, the cash value has become $300. The death benefit is still the same $1,000, but now includes the $300 of forced savings. Therefore, your actual protection is now $700, the difference between the face value ($1,000) and the cash value ($300). Each year that you pay the premiums, the cash value increases and becomes an ever-larger portion of the death benefit.

In other words, permanent life insurance is a combination of decreasing term insurance and increasing cash value. If you live long enough and pay the premiums long enough, *you* will end up supplying the entire death benefit *yourself* because the cash value will then equal the face amount. You would be more of an insurance company that the company itself. But *you* are the premium payer, not the company.

WHAT IS DECREASING TERM INSURANCE?

A type of pure protection life insurance in which the death benefit reduces at scheduled intervals such as every month or every year (monthly decreasing term or annually decreasing term). At the end of a stated period of time (twenty years, age 65, etc.) the policy expires. Critics of decreasing term sometimes refer to it as "disappearing term," because it eventually disappears. However, many of these anti-term salesmen don't bother to tell you that you are buying decreasing term to age 100 when you buy whole life insurance. Or that you can buy decreasing term to age 100 as a separate policy for about half the premium of whole life.

WHAT IS LEVEL TERM INSURANCE?

A type of term insurance in which the death benefit remains constant or "level" for a specified period of time such as to age 65 or 75 or for a certain number of years.

There are two varieties of level term. In one, the premium remains the same for the life of the policy. This is identified as "level-premium level-term." In the second, the premium increases at specified intervals (one year, five years, ten years) This is "increasing-premium level-term" and is usually referred to as "renewable" term. Term insurance may be renewable only, convertible only, or both renewable and convertible.

WHAT DO YOU MEAN BY "RENEWABLE"?

Renewable insurance can be continued in force for a given number of years or to a specified age such as 65, 70, or 75. The company cannot cancel the policy prior to this stated time as long as you pay the premiums. Neither can it require a new physical examination to prove that you are insurable. You are thus guaranteed the right to keep the policy in force regardless of your physical condition.

Premiums for renewable level term increase as you get older. Future premiums are shown in the policy, are guaranteed and cannot be increased above the amounts shown just because you are in poor health or for any other reason. To repeat, only you can cancel a renewable term policy before the expiration date stated in the policy.

NOTE: Premiums for decreasing term do not increase after you have bought such a policy, and the company must permit you to keep it in force to the scheduled expiration date. Both level and decreasing term plans may be considered "renewable."

WHAT DO YOU MEAN BY "CONVERTIBLE"?

Convertible insurance can be exchanged for another insurance plan. Both level and decreasing term plans may have this option to exchange or "convert" to another form of insurance. Some decreasing term plans are convertible to level term, but most companies permit you to convert only to permanent insurance. The conversion option usually expires at age 60, but some plans permit conversion until age 65 or 70. In most term plans, conversion is guaranteed regardless of physical condition. This is an extremely valuable feature since it assures you that you can buy insurance even though you are in poor health. If your term policy was originally issued at standard rates (no extra charge for physical defects), you are guaranteed the right to convert at standard rates.

Most companies permit conversion at either original age (when the policy was first issued) or at present (attained) age. If you convert at original age, you pay a lower premium, but have to make up the difference in premium plus interest. This is usually too costly. Converting at present age means a higher premium per $1,000, but is usually a better choice than conversion at original age. The key feature of convertible term is *conversion without evidence of insurability*. Just be sure that your policy has this provision.

Another feature to look for is the percentage that is convertible, especially in decreasing term plans. It should provide for 100% of the amount in force at time of conversion. Some companies permit less than 100%, so keep your eyes open and know what you are buying.

NOTE: A common practice of some salesmen is to sell you convertible term first and then later try to persuade you to convert to that wonderful permanent insurance. The name of the game is "Second sale, second (and higher) commission." Don't let yourself be trapped. A decreasing term plan that is convertible to level term could be beneficial in case you should need level coverage in the future.

WHAT IS "WHOLE LIFE"?

Whole life is the most common form of permanent insurance. It is a combination of decreasing term to age 100 plus 2½% to 3½% savings account (cash value).* It is also called "straight life," "ordinary life," "life paid up at age 90," and "life paid up at age 95," to name but a few of several designations. Whatever it's called the premium the company charges is based on the assumption that you will pay this same amount your whole life. Since the premium is calculated to be paid over your entire lifetime (not to age 65, for example), the rate for whole life is the lowest of all permanent plans, but still much higher than for pure protection term insurance. If you decide you must have permanent insurance, whole life is your best choice, but it's still no bargain.

WHAT IS "LIMITED-PAYMENT" LIFE INSURANCE?

Limited-payment life is a more costly form of permanent insurance than whole life. Limited-payment life is sold

---

*I don't know of any company that offers a higher percentage, so be careful when your insurance salesman promises all sorts of "goodies."

under various titles: ten-payment life, twenty-payment life, thirty-payment life, life paid up at age 65. Whole life is sometimes called "life paid up at age 95", meaning that premiums are payable to age 95. Obviously, when you cram a lifetime of premiums into a shorter period (such as twenty years or to age 65), the charge per $1,000 of death benefit must be increased to compensate for the shorter premium period. The rule to remember is: "The shorter the payment period, the greater the premium per $1,000." These plans are a poor buy because you get even less protection per premium dollar than from whole life, which isn't exactly a "best buy" either.

NOTE: Don't let yourself be conned into buying a limited-payment policy by the salesman who tells you "Just think! No more premiums after twenty years." Even after you stop paying premiums, you would still be paying through the nose for protection. A so-called "paid-up" policy is one of the most costly you can have. More about this later.

WHAT IS AN "ENDOWMENT" POLICY?

An endowment policy is an even more costly form of permanent insurance than the limited-payment life plans. In an endowment policy, the emphasis is on accumulating a given amount of money within a specified time period. For example, a $1,000 twenty-year endowment will provide $1,000 in cash at the end of twenty years and a death benefit of $1,000 if you die during the twenty years. When analyzed, you find that this is a combination of twenty-year decreasing term plus a savings account that "gallops" along at 2½% to 3½% per year. At the end of twenty years, the policy matures or "endows." At this point, the cash value is $1,000; the decreasing term (protection) is zero. If you were to die, the entire death benefit would be your own money. If you cashed it in for $1,000 you would find that your profit is only slightly more than if you had stuffed the premium money into your mattress. It earns nothing in the mattress, but only slightly more when given to an insurance company. In short, endowment insurance is a costly and unproductive way to accumulate money. Don't buy it!

NOTE: Many parents have bought endowment policies maturing at age 18 for their children's education and have been very disillusioned to find that this tremendous savings program provided about one semester's tuition. Benefit from *their* sad experience, not your own.

WHAT IS "RETIREMENT INCOME INSURANCE"?

Retirement income insurance is the most costly of all permanent insurance plans as far as death benefit per premium dollar is concerned. (It's a poor investment as well). This type is usually sold in units that provide $1,000 of initial death benefit and a retirement income of $10 per month. A retirement income policy at age 65, for example, would have a beginning death benefit of $1,000 and a guaranteed cash value of about $1,500 at age 65. (This is the approximate amount of money an insurance company requires to provide a lifetime income of $10 per month for a sixty-five-year-old man.)

When you reached 50 or 55, such a policy would have a cash value of about $1,000. At this point, the death benefit is entirely your own money and the insurance company no longer has any risk whatsoever. You are still paying the same premium as when you started, but for what?

Here is a diagram of a typical retirement income at age 65 plan:

$1,500

DECREASING TERM
TO AGE 55

CASH VALUE

AGE   35   55   65

As you can see, this is a combination of decreasing term to age 55 plus that wondrous savings account that transfers the death risk from the insurance company to you. The company is very generous, however. Once the cash value equals $1,000, from then on the company agrees that the death benefit will be the full amount of the cash value. If you decide that retirement income insurance is the answer for you, you can bet that your friendly insurance salesman will welcome you with open arms.

NOTE: If you are a self-employed person and have established a Self-Employed Retirement Plan that includes any form of permanent life insurance, you had better reevaluate your program. It's amazing how many otherwise knowledgeable people get trapped into buying a 2½% to 3½% savings plan with the expectations of having adequate retirement income when we are now experiencing double-digit inflation.

To repeat, *term insurance is a part of whatever form of life insurance you may now have or buy in the future*. The preceding discussion was presented in a sequence of progressively more costly forms of life insurance plans. Whole life is lowest premium of the permanent plans, retirement income the highest. To show this relationship in dollars and cents, here are some typical annual premiums per $1,000 for each of these types. As you study these figures, keep in mind that term plans are pure protection, and that permanent insurance is simply a combination of term insurance and a miserably unproductive savings plan.

	Typical Annual Premiums Per $1,000		
Term Plans	Age 35	Age 40	Age 45
Decreasing term to age 65	$ 3.92	$ 4.86	$ 6.15
5-yr renewable & convertible	3.09	4.25	6.62
Level term to age 65	9.76	11.78	14.16
Decreasing term to age 100	8.55	10.90	14.21
Level term to age 75	13.00	16.09	20.00
Permanent Plans			
Whole life	17.55	21.57	26.44
20-payment life	25.50	29.75	34.80
20-year endowment	42.00	43.20	45.00
Retirement income at age 65	36.20	47.74	65.50

You don't have to be an Einstein to understand why permanent insurance is pushed by most companies and salesmen.

CHAPTER THREE

MORE INSURANCE JARGON

Like any other business, the life insurance industry uses language and terminology that has definite and established meanings. Words like "renewable," "convertible," "insurability" and others were explained in the preceding chapter. There are others that you should know and understand in order to evaluate your present life insurance program or to buy additional life insurance.

Let's start with a discussion of "mutual" and "stock"—the two main types of life insurance companies in business today.

A stock company is a corporation owned by the investors who had bought shares of the company's stock either when it was first formed, or at some later date. As stockholders they have a financial interest in the company and expect to receive income and profits from their investments. Officers of the company are elected by the shareholders and may be removed and replaced if enough stockholders become dissatisfied with the progress of the company. This scrutiny by the stockholders (owners) keeps management on its toes, and consequently the stock life insurance companies are reasonably efficient operations.

A mutual life insurance company is owned by the policyholders. At least, this is the theory. In reality, it is a company with no stockholders asking questions about how your money is spent. With no stockholders to report to or be concerned about, a mutual company can perpetuate an inefficient management for years! Directors pick the officers, and the officers select the directors. Mutual companies tend to be loosely operated and inefficient. Their operating expenses are usually substantially higher than those of stock companies of comparable size.

NOTE: If you are a policyholder of a mutual company, you are eligible to attend the annual meeting. If you should decide to attend, you would discover that you would have about as much influence as the janitor who cleans the company's plush, high-rise office building.

WHAT IS PARTICIPATING INSURANCE?

Participating insurance is the type sold by mutual companies and some stock companies. As a holder of a participating or "par" policy, you are entitled to receive policy dividends. You are told that these are your share of the company's profits. The truth is that your so-called "dividend" is nothing more than a partial refund of an intentional overcharge included in the premium. When you buy a par policy, either term or permanent, the premium you pay includes an overcharge of 20%, 30%, or more. (See Table I in the Appendix)

WHAT IS NON-PARTICIPATING INSURANCE?

Insurance that does not pay dividends. It is also referred to as "guaranteed premium" and "non-par." It is sold by most stock companies and some mutual companies. Since non-par premiums include no overcharge for future refunds (dividends), you get more protection per premium dollar from non-par than from par plans. The typical premiums listed in the preceding chapter are all non-par. Fortunately, life insurance buyers are beginning to question the value of overpriced participating insurance and are now purchasing more of the lower cost, non-par plans than in previous years. Be sure that you buy this type from a stock company only!

WHAT ARE NONFORFEITURE VALUES?

Briefly, nonforfeiture values are guaranteed options available to you if you decide to stop paying premiums on a policy, or want to use the money accumulated within a policy. Nonforfeiture values are required by law in all permanent plans and are found in some term plans. Here is a typical nonforfeiture table of a non-par whole life policy issued at age 30, (with an annual premium of $14.45 per $1000):

Policy Year	Cash or Loan Value	Paid-Up Value	Extended Term Yrs.	Days
1	0	0	0	0
2	0	0	0	0
3	9	26	2	341
4	23	64	6	267
5	37	101	9	167
6	51	135	11	169
7	66	171	13	38
8	81	204	14	117
9	96	236	15	89
10	111	266	15	344
11	128	299	16	232
12	145	331	17	58
13	162	361	17	194
14	180	392	17	315
15	198	421	18	31
16	216	448	18	78
17	234	474	18	98
18	253	501	18	114
19	272	527	18	107
20	291	551	18	81
Age				
55	379	646	17	10
60	468	723	15	185
65	555	787	13	302

The key figure is the amount in the column headed "Cash or Loan Value" since all other values are based on this amount. You will note that this is zero until the third policy year. Therefore, this policy, like most all permanent plans, would have no salvage or surrender value until premiums had been paid for three years. This is the result of "front-loading" which means that all of your premiums for the first two years are used by the company and none of this money is credited to the cash value. Finally in the third year, a portion of the premium is shown as cash value.

The annual premium per $1,000 for this particular whole-life policy is $14.45 at age 30. In comparison, this same company sells five-year renewable and convertible level term for $2.45 per $1,000. This is a difference of $12.00 per year per $1,000.

If you were this thirty-year-old, you could have either

saved $12.00 per year and thus avoided the front-loaded whole-life plan, or you could have bought almost $6,000 of pure protection term insurance for the $14.45 charged for $1,000 of whole-life. That's quite a difference, isn't it!

Getting back to the nonforfeiture values, let's look at the tenth year values:

Cash or loan value	$111
Paid-up value	$266
Extended term value	15 years, 344 days

These figures mean that at the end of ten years, you could:

1. Cancel the policy and receive $111 in cash.
2. Borrow the $111 and pay 5% per year on the loan.
3. Stop paying premiums and have $266 of insurance for the rest of your life.
4. Stop paying premiums and have $1,000 of insurance for 15 years, 344 days.

Now let's examine these options.

Cash Surrender

If you exercised this choice, you would have $111 in cash and no insurance.

Borrow the cash value

This choice would cost you $5.55 per year to use your own money and would reduce the death benefit of your policy to $889. You would continue to pay the premium of $14.45 plus $5.55 interest for a total cost of $20.00 per year. You are not required to repay the loan if you choose not to. However, if you die before the loan is repaid, your beneficiary would receive only $889, the difference between the face amount ($1,000 and the loan of $111).

NOTE: The cash or loan value is also the amount that you are contributing to the total death benefit. At the ten-year point, it's only $111, but at age 65 you would be supplying 55.5% of the total death benefit and the company would be taking only 44.5% of the risk.

Convert to paid-up insurance

This choice would eliminate all future premiums and

you would have $266 of life insurance for as long as you lived. Sounds attractive? Don't be too sure.

Of the $266 of death benefit, $111 of it would be your own money. The difference between $266 and $111 is $155, which is the amount of true protection you would have. You would pay no premiums, but you would be losing the interest that the $111 would earn. Even at 5%, you would be losing $5.55 per year. Therefore, you would be paying $5.55 per year for $155 of insurance, or $35.81 per $1,000. ($5.55 divided by .155).

If you had bought this whole life policy at age 30 and are now age 40, you can buy five-year renewable and convertible level term for $4.25 per $1000. In other words, the interest that you would be losing would more than pay the premium for $1,000 of honest protection.

If you question these calculations, go ahead, convert to paid-up insurance, borrow the $111 at 5% and then die. You won't know about it, but your widow may be rather unhappy to receive only $155 after the company deducted your $111 loan from the $266 face amount. Paid-up insurance isn't much of a bargain, is it?

NOTE: If you have been led to believe that you can have both your money *and* your protection, take another look. It's a matter of protection *or* money. You don't have this problem with term insurance.

If you have been feeling self-satisfied and complacent about your paid-up policies, you had better get them out of their hiding place and see what they are really costing you. The same analysis applies to these supposed treasures.

Convert to extended term insurance

This option would permit you to stop paying premiums and have $1,000 of insurance for 15 years, 344 days. At the end of this period, the policy would expire without value.

Selecting the extended term value would tie up your $111 of cash surrender value. Unlike the paid-up option, you cannot borrow the money once you have elected to convert to extended term. You are usually permitted to change your mind at a later date and get back a portion of the money, but you cannot borrow it.

Now let's look at the arithmetic involved. In return for leaving your $111 with the company, you would have $1,000 of insurance for practically 16 years. This averages out to $6.94 per year ($111 divided by 16 years). This is less than the $14.45 whole-life premium and substantially less than the cost of $35.81 per $1000 of the paid up option. But, don't conclude that this is a sound choice, either.

At age 40 (your present age assuming you bought the whole life policy ten years ago at age 30), you can buy five-year renewable and convertible level term for $4.25 per $1,000. The premiums increase at five-year intervals as follows:

Age 40-44	$ 4.25
Age 45-49	$ 6.57
Age 50-54	$ 9.89
Age 55	$14.95

NOTE: Isn't it interesting that at age 55 you can buy insurance for only slightly more than the whole-life policy you bought at age 30?

Now that you have purchased the term insurance, you cancel the old policy and put the $111 in the bank at 5% interest. If you should die, your widow would receive the $111 plus the insurance of $1,000. Right? In the meantime, you would receive $5.55 per year in interest. To keep it simple, we will forget about compounding and just figure a constant $5.55 per year. Here is the sixteen-year summary:

Interest on $111 @ 5% for 16 years @ $5.55 per year		$ 88.80
Term insurance premiums		
5 years @ $4.25 per year	$21.25	
5 years @ $6.57 per year	32.85	
5 years @ $9.89 per year	49.45	
1 year @ $14.95 per year	14.95	
Total insurance premiums (16 years)		$118.50
Difference between premiums paid and interest earned		$ 29.70

Over the sixteen years, you would have paid out $29.70 more for insurance than your former cash value earned at 5%. Let's assume that you paid this amount from some other source. After paying yourself back, you would end up with $81.30. ($111 less $29.70). In comparison, the extended term option would have used up the entire $111.

The renewable term policy you bought at age 40 could be renewed to your age 70 if you so desired. The extended term coverage would end after 15 years, 344 days at your age 56.

NOTE: This explanation of nonforfeiture values was based on a $1,000 policy to keep the arithmetic at a reasonable level. The same analysis would apply to any permanent policy, regardless of face amount. Don't dismiss this discussion as unimportant just because small figures were used for illustration.

WHAT IS A MORTALITY TABLE?

A mortality table is a record of *past* death rates used by life insurance companies to calculate *present* premiums to cover possible *future* death claims. A mortality table shows the anticipated death rate per 1,000 people by age, and their average life expectancy.

For example:

Age	Death Rate Per 1000	Life Expectancy
25	1.93	45.82 years
30	2.13	41.25 years
35	2.51	36.69 years

The death rate per 1,000 is the basis of the premium charged by a life insurance company. To this basic figure is added other amounts needed to cover the costs of issuing a policy, possible lapses, operating expenses, company profits plus any other "contingent" costs the company may decide is necessary.

Since 1966, all life companies have used the 1958 mortality table which shows the death rates of 1950-54. Prior to 1966, most companies used the 1941 version, a record of the death rates of the 1930s. (We didn't even have penicillin in those days, and the death rate was much higher than at present.) However, the real shocker is the fact that there are policies in force today based on the American Experience Table and the death rates of 1843-1858. This is pre-Civil War!

The older tables show a much higher death rate than the newer ones. When such obsolete information is used as a starting point for calculating premiums, the resulting premiums are higher than necessary to cover mortality costs and you, the buyer, are being overcharged. Here is a brief comparison of three tables mentioned above along with the *actual* death rate in the United States for 1959-61:

Death Rates Per 1000

Age	American Experience (1843-58)	Commissioners 1941 Table (1930-40)	Commissioners 1958 Table (1950-54)	U.S. Death Rate (1959-61)
25	8.06	2.43	1.79	1.15
30	8.43	3.56	2.13	1.43
35	8.95	4.59	2.51	1.94
40	9.79	6.18	3.53	3.00
45	11.16	8.61	5.35	4.76
50	13.78	12.32	8.32	7.74
55	18.57	17.98	13.00	11.61
60	26.69	26.59	20.34	17.61
65	40.13	39.64	31.75	26.22

The table used by the company when you bought your policy is under the heading "Basis of Computation" or similar title. Get your policies out and see what you have. If the table is other than the 1958 model, you have a real relic. This section of your policy also gives the interest rate for the cash value of the policy.

NOTE: If you bought a policy at age 30 based on the 1941 death rate of 3.56 deaths per 1,000 and are now age 40, you will note that the 1958 death rate for your present age is only 3.53 per 1,000 and that the most recent U.S. death rate is only 3.00 per 1,000. But your premiums are still based on the death rate of the 1930s! If you feel this is unfair, consider the fact that at age 40, you can now buy annually renewable term for $3.22 per $1,000. Does this strike a nerve? For ages other than 40, consult Appendix Table III.

33

WHAT IS WAIVER OF PREMIUM?

Waiver of premium is a low-cost option that provides for payment of your insurance premium by the company if you become totally and completely disabled. Most companies require that you be disabled for at least six months before this provision takes effect; some require only four months.

Waiver of premium coverage usually expires at age 60, so your disability must start before this age. If you become disabled before age 60, the company will continue to pay the premiums beyond age 60 if you are still disabled. Some companies include waiver of premium coverage in the basic premium; others make a separate charge. It is inexpensive and is available with term insurance.

NOTE: Waiver of premium coverage for term plans normally provides for payment of premiums until the scheduled expiration of the term policy. Some companies provide for automatic conversion to whole life if disabled, with the company continuing to pay the whole-life premium as long as you are disabled. This broader coverage costs a little more, but is still a good buy.

Remember that waiver of premium coverage provides only for payment of the premiums while you are disabled. It does not pay you anything in cash. If you would also need income while you are disabled, you should buy disability income insurance. This is a subject in itself and will not be discussed in this book.

WHAT IS ACCIDENTAL DEATH BENEFIT?

Accidental death benefit is an extra item that may be added to a life insurance plan or bought separately. It provides an additional amount of money for your beneficiary if your death is due to accident, rather than natural causes, before age 65 or 70. It is also known as "double indemnity," since the total death benefit for accidental death is twice the face amount of the policy. Some companies offer "triple indemnity" (three times the face amount) in case you are killed while a fare-paying passenger in a public carrier (train, plane, bus, etc.). ADB is available with both level- and decreasing-term plans, but not from all companies. When ADB is added to decreasing-term plans, the ADB coverage portion remains constant.

NOTE: The cost of ADB is fairly low, but is a somewhat questionable benefit. It often gives a false sense of security because you are apt to feel that your family will get this extra money since you "know" that you will die accidentally. Don't be so sure that your death will be accidental, that you ask your family to depend on this coverage for money to live on. Pure protection term insurance is very inexpensive, pays off for death from any cause and you should not expect your family to rely on a possible accidental death.

WHAT IS MEANT BY "CONTESTABILITY"?

Contestability is a standard provision of all life insurance policies that protects the insurance companies from dishonest or unscrupulous buyers. This clause provides that if you die within two years because of a physical condition or personal activity that you knowingly concealed from the insurance company when you applied for the insurance, the company does not have to pay the face amount of the policy. The company must prove that you willfully and knowingly concealed this information and that this withheld information was responsible for your death. After two years, the policy is no longer contestable and the company must pay off, regardless of how you died, even if you committed suicide.

To illustrate, you might have a heart condition and conceal this fact from the company. If you were to have a heart attack and die within two years and if it could be established that you knew you had a bad heart, the company would merely refund the premiums you had paid. If you lived beyond the two years, you would be fully covered.

Another situation might be that you were a scuba diver, didn't tell the company and then drowned while scuba diving. Your family would receive only a refund of the premiums.

NOTE: Salesmen have been known to "rattle the contestable clause" to keep you from dropping the policy they had previously sold to you. By implying that a new insurance policy would not pay off if you were to die within two years, they try to scare you into continuing their policy. If this should happen to you, don't let it bother you. As long as you are honest, answer all questions truthfully and conceal nothing, the contestable clause is no problem.

WHAT IS "GUARANTEED INSURABILITY BENEFIT"?

Guaranteed insurability benefit is also known as "guaranteed purchase option. Whatever it's called, it boils down to an extra-charge item that permits you to buy additional insurance in the future without having to take a physical or otherwise prove that you are physically qualified for insurance. It normally permits you to buy a specified amount of new insurance at certain ages. For example, at age 25 you could add a guaranteed insurability benefit to a policy that would enable you to buy more insurance without examination at ages 28, 31, 34 and 37.

Nearly all companies require that you buy some form of *permanent* insurance at the beginning and that you buy only *additional permanent* insurance when you exercise the options. However, at least one company, Occidental Life of California will sell you five-year renewable and convertible term as a starter and then let you add a rider to guarantee you the right to buy $15,000 more of the same five-year convertible and renewable term at three-year intervals. If you start at age 25 with $25,000 and then add $15,000 at ages 28, 31, 34, and 37, you will have $85,000 at age 37.

If you are concerned about your future insurability, this benefit can be very useful. Just don't let yourself be talked into buying permanent insurance. You can start with low-cost protection and continue to buy the same.

NOTE: The deposit term plan offered by University Life in Indianapolis which is discussed in a subsequent chapter also permits you to buy a guaranteed insurability rider.

CHAPTER FOUR

VARIETIES OF TERM LIFE INSURANCE

Now that you have learned some of the definitions and translations of life insurance terminology, we can dig a little deeper and examine the various forms of term life insurance. It would be so simple if all companies got together and decided to sell only a specific number or types of life insurance instead of the confusing conglomeration now offered to life insurance buyers. It's doubtful if any such standardization will ever occur. The only solution is for you to become acquainted with the different types so that you can make an intelligent selection.

ARE ALL DECREASING TERM PLANS THE SAME?

No, they are similar, but not identical. The most obvious difference is the period of time covered, which may be as brief as five years or may extend to your age 100. The most common form is decreasing term to age 65, since this is the anticipated retirement age for most people. You may also buy decreasing term to age 70 or 75. As a general rule, you should buy term to at least age 65.

A second variable is the rate of decrease over the life of the policy. Some plans reduce monthly; some yearly. Some stay level for the first three or four years and then start reducing each month or year.

One of the most common forms is "straight-line" or "uniformly" decreasing term. This type reduces at the same rate each year. For example, a twenty-five-year straight-line decreasing term policy reduces at a constant 4% per year. A forty-year plan would reduce at a constant 2½% per year. A straight-line plan may also have a "level-off" feature in which the coverage stops reducing in the last four or five years. This level coverage is normally 20% of the starting amount. Appendix Table VI lists typical premiums for this type of term insurance.

A second form of decreasing term is "mortgage term" which reduces very gradually since it is designed to coincide with paying off a mortgage. As you are well aware, a mortgage reduces very slowly in the early years because only a portion of your payment is applied to the principal.

Most mortgage term plans are based on a 6% mortgage. If your loan rate is more than 6% and you want to fully cover your mortgage balance, you will need to buy more coverage at the beginning. Otherwise, your insurance coverage will reduce faster than your mortgage. A few companies are now offering mortgage insurance based on a 7½% loan. Be sure you know what you are buying.

A third form of decreasing term is "family income term." This is often sold in units that provide $10 per month of income for a given period of time. Each unit of $10 per month of income is equivalent to these amounts of protection:

$10 Per month for this many years	Insurance Value
35 years	$2,621
30 years	2,391
25 years	2,124
20 years	1,815
15 years	1,456
10 years	1,041

Family income term reduces more rapidly than mortgage term, but not as fast as straight-line term. It's probably easier to think of it as "in-between" term because its reduction rate is in-between the other two types. To give you an idea of the relative rate of decrease, here is a comparison of four decreasing term plans:

Policy Year	Mortgage term (7½%)	Mortgage term (6%)	In-between term	Straight-line term
1	$1,000	$1,000	$1,000	$1,000
5	959	946	912	867
10	887	856	786	700
15	781	736	641	533
20	628	576	472	367
25	405	358	276	200
30	200	65	50	33*

*Straight-line term with the level-off feature would remain at 200 for the last six years.

NOTE: The premium per $1,000 for the 7½% mortgage term is the highest since it reduces the most slowly. The straight-line premium is the lowest since the coverage reduces the most rapidly. For a given amount of premium, you will obtain more *initial* protection with straight-line than with any of the other types. The key point to remember is not to expect $25,000 of straight-line term to fully cover a $25,000 mortgage. The Appendix includes additional discussion of this subject.

ARE ALL LEVEL TERM PLANS THE SAME?

No, but they are all similar in that they provide a constant or level amount of protection for a stated number of years or to a given age such as age 65 or 75. Renewable level term was explained earlier and it was pointed out that premiums increase with each renewal. Not all renewable term plans are renewable to age 65 or 70; some are renewable for only ten years, for example. This type isn't a very good buy. You may think ten years will be enough, but your plans may change. If you still need insurance after ten years, but are in poor health, you might be unable to get insurance or have to pay an extra charge for a "rated" policy. A plan that is renewable to age 65 or 70 without evidence of insurability is a far better buy.

In a level-premium level-term plan (no increases in premium), you overpay in the early years in order to avoid increased premiums in later years. The overpayment builds up a reserve (cash value) in the policy which is used to offset the higher mortality costs as you become older. When the policy expires, this reserve is completely used up. A diagram of a typical level-premium level-term policy would look like this:

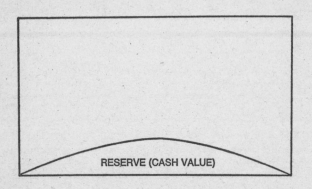

RESERVE (CASH VALUE)

NOTE: Even though a level premium level term plan includes a cash value similar to permanent insurance, it should not be considered a savings plan. The cash value in this case is solely a mathematical means of providing level protection for a constant premium. Level term plans of fifteen years or longer usually have a cash value.

SINCE THE PREMIUMS FOR RENEWABLE TERM INCREASE AS I GET OLDER, WON'T I BE PAYING MORE FOR MY INSURANCE IN LATER YEARS?

You are going to pay more for your protection as you get older regardless of the type of policy you buy. This may not fit in with what you have probably been told, but it is a fact that you need to understand. When you buy a decreasing term policy, your premium remains constant but your protection decreases. Thus, when you divide the premium by the amount of coverage, you find that the cost per $1,000 of protection increases. For example, at age 35, you can buy thirty-year straight-line decreasing term for $3.61 per $1,000. This is how the cost per $1,000 would increase:

Policy Year	Your Age	Amount of Insurance	Annual Premium	Actual Cost Per $1,000
1	35	$1,000	$3.61	$ 3.61
5	40	867	3.61	4.16
10	45	700	3.61	5.16
15	50	533	3.61	6.77
20	55	367	3.61	9.84
25	60	200	3.61	18.05

Now let's examine a permanent insurance plan, such as non-par whole life bought at age 35 for an annual premium of $17.55 per $1,000. First, compare this figure with the last column in the above tabulation. You will note that at age 60, your actual cost per $1,000 of insurance is only slightly more than the whole-life premium for age 35. Interesting, isn't it?

Keep in mind that the whole-life premium includes an extra amount over and above the cost of protection that will eventually be credited to the cash value of the policy. Also remember that each increase in cash value *reduces the true amount of insurance you have* and that *you are* losing the earning power of this accumulated cash value. Here is how this whole-life policy bought at age 35 would look in later years:

Policy Year	Your Age	Cash Value	Actual Insurance	Lost Interest @ 5%	Total Cost*	Cost Per $1,000
1	35	—	$1,000	—	$17.55	$17.55
5	40	$ 48	952	$ 2.40	19.95	20.95
10	45	135	865	6.75	24.30	28.09
15	50	232	768	11.60	29.15	37.96
20	55	334	666	16.70	34.25	51.89
25	60	430	570	21.50	39.05	68.51

*Premium of $17.55 plus lost interest.

Your question concerned the higher premiums of renewable term. For a further comparison, here are the annual premiums per $1,000 for five-year renewable and convertible starting at age 35:

Your Age	Premium Per $1,000
35	$ 3.09
40	4.20
45	6.57
50	9.89
55	14.95
60	24.48

Now compare the figures in the column headed "Lost Interest," which is calculated as 5% of the cash value of the whole-life policy. You will note that from age 45 on, the lost interest *alone* would pay the premium for five-year renewable and convertible term. At age 60, the lost interest is slightly less ($21.50 vs. $24.48). However, don't forget that these figures do not include the whole-life premium of $17.55, or the additional benefit of compounding the interest each year.

NOTE: Many salesmen try to discourage people from buying renewable term by overemphasizing the higher premiums at older ages. Now that you know how to determine the true cost of protection, don't let this scare technique push you into overpriced permanent insurance.

WOULD IT BE ADVISABLE TO BUY RENEWABLE LEVEL TERM RATHER THAN DECREASING TERM?

It's a point to consider. A definite advantage of renewable level term is that you control the amount of coverage. A decreasing term plan reduces at a scheduled rate which may not fit your financial situation in later years. With renewable term you can maintain the same amount that you start with or can renew only the amount you need. This flexibility is very helpful since you cannot be absolutely certain of future financial requirements.

WHAT IS "DEPOSIT TERM"?

This is a relatively new product of the life insurance industry and one that is attracting a great amount of interest. A typical deposit term is a ten-year level term policy that may be renewed for additional ten-year periods or converted to decreasing term to age 100. It differs from other term plans in that your first year's premium includes a deposit which is your pledge that you will keep the policy in force for at least ten years. If you keep your promise, your deposit is refunded to you plus interest at 10% per year compounded annually. This is a tax-free refund.

If you die before the ten years is up, the deposit is paid to your beneficiary. If you break your promise and drop the policy before the ten years is up, you forfeit your deposit. Here are typical annual premiums, first-year deposits and tenth-year refunds:

Issue Age	Annual Premium	First-Year Deposit	Tenth-Year Refund
25	$ 3.05	$ 6.17	$16.00
30	3.62	6.94	18.00
35	4.68	7.32	19.00
40	6.41	8.10	21.00
45	8.89	9.64	25.00
50	12.32	11.57	30.00
55	18.00	13.49	35.00
60	29.00	16.95	44.00

WHAT HAPPENS AT THE END OF TEN YEARS?

1. You can collect the tax-free refund and drop the policy.
2. You can collect the tax-free refund and renew the policy for another ten years, either the full amount or a lesser amount. The premium would be based on your new age, and you would make a new deposit for that age.
3. You can collect the tax-free refund and convert the policy to decreasing term to age 100.
4. You can convert the policy to whole life. With this option, you do not receive the refund. Instead, this money becomes a part of the cash value of the whole-life policy.

NOTE: Some deposit term plans do not permit conversion to decreasing term to age 100; only to whole life. Avoid a plan such as this.

WHAT ARE THE SPECIAL ADVANTAGES OF DEPOSIT TERM?

Since it is a level term plan, your coverage does not reduce unless you want it to. The premium is lower than most ten-year renewable and convertible term policies. The tax-free 10% return on your deposit is guaranteed and further reduces the cost of protection. The policy is convertible to decreasing term to age 100, whereas most renewable term plans are renewable only to age 70 or 75. The first-year premium (including the deposit) is less than for whole life. If you should die within the ten years, your beneficiary receives the deposit. (Remember that the extra premium charged for a whole-life policy is used by the company; don't forget the front-loading mentioned earlier.) Both renewal as level term and conversion to decreasing term are guaranteed regardless of your physical condition.

NOTE: Deposit term may be described as low-cost level protection plus a guaranteed 10% tax-free investment. If you are certain you can earn more than 10% per year on your money, you should forget about deposit term.

CAN YOU ILLUSTRATE A $100,000 DEPOSIT TERM PLAN FOR AGE 45?

	Ages 45 thru 54	Ages 55 thru 64
Face amount	$100,000	$100,000
Add deposit	964	1,349
Total death benefit	$100,964	$101,349
First-year premium	$ 1,853	$ 3,149
Premium for years 2-10 and 12-20	889	1,800
Total premiums and deposits per 10 years	8,965	17,549
Less Tenth and Twentieth-year refunds	2,500	3,500
Net cost of protection	6,465	14,049
Average annual cost per $1,000 of protection	$6.47	$14.05

At the end of twenty years (age 65) you could convert to decreasing term to age 100. The maximum amount would be $56,700 and the maximum premium would be $1,800. You could also collect the tax-free $3,500 and drop the policy.

In comparison, $100,000 of whole life (non-par) bought at age 45 would cost about $2,500 per year, or $50,000 for twenty years. In case of your death, your family would receive no more from the whole-life plan than from the deposit-term policy. However, you would have paid almost 2½ times as much in total premiums ($20,514 for twenty years of deposit term vs. $50,000 for whole life).

The whole-life policy would have a cash value at age 65 of about $40,000, and therefore a true protection of only $60,000. If you wanted to use the $40,000 you would either have to pay interest of $2,000 per year (5% of $40,000) or cancel the policy. With the deposit term plan, you would save close to $30,000 in premiums. This amount of money could be invested very conservatively and easily exceed the $40,000 cash value of the whole-life plan.

CHAPTER FIVE

THE BAIT OF "SOMETHING BACK"

The husband and father who buys term insurance on his life is a very unselfish person. His only concern is the welfare of his family in case of his death. He doesn't ask: "What do *I* get back?" or "What is there in it for *me?*" He knows that term insurance is pure protection and pays off only if he dies while the policy is in force. He understands that the payoff is to his widow and children, not to him. He expects nothing in return for his premiums other than the personal satisfaction of knowing that his family has substantially more protection than if he were spending the same amount of premium for permanent insurance.

NOTE: A thirty-year-old father with $200 per year to spend for life insurance has these choices:

$77,551 of five-year renewable and convertible level term

$58,462 of decreasing term to age 65

$27,941 of decreasing term to age 100

$23,059 of level premium level term to age 65

$13,149 of whole life

$11,059 of life paid up at age 65

$6,022 of retirement income at age 65

(These figures are based on the non-par premiums of Old Line Life)

It's difficult—if not impossible—to be completely unselfish. Regardless of who we are, we are going to consider our own desires. How much we emphasize our personal preferences becomes a measure of our selfishness or unselfishness. The life insurance industry is well aware of our innate self-interest and has capitalized on it unmercifully, because it is a greedy and selfish industry.

Death is a morbid and distasteful subject, one that we dislike to even think or talk about. Some salesmen still "back the hearse up to the door" with pictures of the father missing from the dinner table, or a bereaved widow at graveside, or some other emotional reminder of death. Even though there are still too many of these hucksters in business today, fortunately their numbers are fading. Instead of painting these woeful pictures of death and its consequences, the pitch has been changed to what you (the buyer) will receive.

"Something back!" How many times have you been told about the tremendous benefits of permanent life insurance? How the cash value and dividends will lower your "net cost"? How this modern miracle will send your kids through college, provide retirement income for you and your wife, pay for that trip around the world, and still leave great gobs of money for your children and grandchildren after you pass on.

Permanent life insurance will do so many things for you that it's completely unthinkable for you to consider anything other than this unbelievable bargain of all bargains. You simply cannot afford to be without it. Just sign here so you can put this wonderful program into effect— RIGHT NOW! Does this sound familiar?

This appeal to our selfish instincts is completely contrary to the basic purpose of life insurance—*protection against the premature death of a person who is responsible for the financial security of others*. Life insurance was not intended to give you—the buyer—something back, and this asinine switch of priorities has made the life insurance industry the richest of all industries at the expense of untold numbers of widows and orphans. The evidence is in the miserable statistics of *The Widows' Study*, and the welfare rolls loaded with widows and orphans just barely existing on Social Security.

NOTE: If you doubt that these conditions exist, take a look around you. Check with some of the widows you know and find out how high on the hog they are living.

Also, if you think your survivors will be financially secure on government welfare, consider the plight of the American Indian.

A favorite device of the cash value advocates is the "Net Cost Method." (Net Cost *Myth* is more appropriate.) This numbers game is designed to prove how inexpensive permanent insurance really is by showing all the "goodies" you get back.

To illustrate this numerical gyration, let's take a $10,000 whole-life policy sold to a man of 35 for an annual premium of $240. This is a par policy, and the dividends (partial refunds of an intentional overcharge) are *guesstimated* to total $1,500 over the next twenty years. The twentieth-year cash value will be $3,610. Here's the arithmetic of the Net Cost myth:

Total premiums for 20 years	$4,800
Less guesstimated dividends (refunds)	−$1,500
Net premiums for 20 years	$3,300
Less 20th year cash value	−$3,610
Net cost	($310)
Average cost per year	($15.50)
Average cost per year per $1,000	($1.55)

Isn't this absolutely unbelievable? $10,000 of insurance for twenty years—and you get all your money back, plus some more. The insurance company is actually giving you free protection. How can you afford to turn down such a deal?

If you are at all concerned about your family's welfare or your pocketbook, you had better turn it down. Here are some of the reasons:

The first and most important reason is that this $240 of premium will buy $68,390 of thirty-year straight-line decreasing term for a thirty-five-year-old. Slight difference in death benefits, isn't there?

A second reason is that dividends are not guaranteed.

By adding the possible dividends into the calculations, the net cost myth implies that dividends are just as certain as the guaranteed cash value. They are not!

A third reason is that you shouldn't buy dividends to begin with. The par premium of $240 includes an overcharge of at least $54.50. A non-par whole life policy from a stock company would cost $185.50 per year. This overcharge of $54.50 figures out to be approximately 29%. If you bought the $10,000 non-par policy, you would have an immediate and guaranteed dividend of $54.50 per year from now on. With the par policy, it would take about eight to ten years before your annual dividend equaled the initial overcharge. In the interim, the insurance company would have the use of your money and wouldn't even have to pay you interest. Wouldn't *you* like to be an insurance company?

If you insisted on buying permanent insurance, your $240 of premium would buy $13,100 of non-par whole life from a stock company. This is 31% more protection for your family than from the par plan. The twentieth-year cash value would be $4,375. This is a guaranteed amount, and would not be dependent upon guesstimated dividends.

NOTE: Don't overlook the fact that as soon as either a par or non-par permanent insurance policy has a cash value, you also have less actual protection *because the cash value is providing part of the death benefit.*

In recent years, the Net Cost Method has been criticized within the life insurance industry because this system includes no consideration for what the premium money would amount to if invested elsewhere. Alternate methods have been proposed, discussed and discarded for one reason or another. The one that has been given the most attention is the "Interest-Adjusted Method." This approach recognizes that money does earn interest unless you stick it under your mattress or in a piggybank. (Quite an amazing and weighty conclusion, isn't it?) The interest rate selected was 4%, a very conservative estimate of what your money might earn in a long term savings account.

Here is the arithmetic of the Interest-Adjusted Method using the same figures as the Net Cost Method:

Total value of $240 per year for 20 years @ 4%	$7,433
Less 20 annual dividends each accumulated @ 4%	−$2,003
Net premiums for 20 years	$5,430
Less 20th-year cash value	−$3,610
Net Insurance cost for 20 years	$1,820

The IAM Cost is determined by dividing $1,820 (Net Insurance Cost) by the factor 30.97, which is the value of one dollar invested at 4% for 20 years. The result is $58.77. When this amount is divided by 10 (for a $10,000 policy), the interested-adjusted cost per $1,000 per year is said to be $5.88.

You will recall that the Net Cost myth produced a "profit" of $1.55 per $1,000 per year. The newer system shows a *cost* of $5.88 per $1,000 per year. Obviously, if there is a cost there can be no profit and it's easy to understand why the Net Cost advocates object to the Interest-Adjusted Method. It knocks their sales presentations into a cocked hat!

The National Association of Insurance Commissioners favors the Interest-Adjusted Method, although it is not a unanimous decision. (NAIC is made up of the fifty different state insurance department commissioners who don't always agree on insurance matters.) It's rather interesting in that the NAIC position is that the Interest-Adjusted Method is not the best system; it's just the least bad.

Another insurance organization, the National Association of Life Underwriters, opposes the Interest-Adjusted Method. Their contention is that it is even more confusing and complex than the Net Cost Method and would not improve the public's understanding of life insurance.

NOTE: NALU is an organization of life insurance salesmen with national, state, and local offices. Most members are outspoken advocates of cash-value life insurance and strive to qualify for the Million Dollar Round Table each year. By selling at least one million dollars of permanent insurance each year, they can enter this elite selling fraternity. Term insurance gives them much less MDRT credit than permanent insurance. You can easily understand why they like cash-value insurance.

Getting back to the Net Cost and Interest-Adjusted methods—both are based on assumptions that are questionable and meaningless:

1. Both assume that the buyer should get "something back" from his insurance premiums. If this is such a valid requirement, why don't the fire insurance companies offer cash values and dividends?

2. Both assume that dividends will materialize as illustrated. Dividends are not guaranteed, and shouldn't be bought to begin with.

3. Both assume that a policy will be surrendered at the end of a stated period of time. What if you still need insurance after twenty years? Remember that you lose your protection the same instant that you surrender a policy for its cash value. You simply *cannot have both protection and money* when you buy only permanent life insurance. If you don't surrender the policy, the cost figures mean absolutely nothing. You have simply overpaid.

4. Both assume that you will be alive at the end of twenty years or whatever period is used. If you know you will be alive this long, why buy any life insurance at all? Just put your money into the bank or government bonds. It will earn at least the 4% implied by the Interest-Adjusted Method, and you won't have to pay 80% or more for a front-loaded whole-life plan and its 2½% to 3½% savings account. In short, why settle for the meager return of cash-value life insurance?

It will be quite some time before the life insurance industry agrees to accept a universal cost method. In the meantime, try this one:

It was mentioned earlier that the $240 you would be charged for a $10,000 participating whole-life policy at age 35 would buy $68,390 of thirty-year straight-line decreasing term or $13,100 of non-par whole life. Let's forget about the par plan and compare only the two non-par policies. This is the "Survivor Cost Method" and illustrates the cost of permanent insurance to your widow and orphans.

Policy Year of Death	Death Benefit of Whole Life	Death Benefit of Decreasing Term	Cost to the Survivors
1	$13,100	$68,390	$55,290
5	13,100	59,294	46,194
10	13,100	47,873	34,773
15	13,100	36,452	23,352
20	13,100	25,100	12,000
25	13,100	13,678	578
30	13,100	13,678	578

The last column on the right is the "real cost" of permanent life insurance—one that is too frequently paid by widows and orphans because Dad was conned into buying cash value and dividends by the fancy figurework of the permanent insurance salesman who was more interested in his commission than the welfare of his client.

Why don't you ask *your* wife which cost method makes the most sense to *her?*

BUT IF I DON'T DIE, I'VE PAID $240 PER YEAR AND GOT NOTHING BACK. WHY NOT BUY THE WHOLE-LIFE POLICY AND TAKE A CHANCE THAT I WILL LIVE LONG ENOUGH TO GET SOMETHING BACK?

Your question is an excellent illustration of how we have been brainwashed by the life insurance industry. By dangling the bait of cash values and dividends, they appeal to your selfishness and lead you into either overpaying for protection or underprotecting your family—very probably both. If you take this bait, you end up in their trap.

To refresh your thinking, let's again review how permanent life insurance works by imagining that the company from which you buy the fire insurance for your home followed the same procedure as the life insurance companies.

You have just bought a new home and you have established that you can buy the amount of fire protection you need for $100 per year. But then the salesman tells you that you would be better off to buy "permanent" coverage because this plan builds up a cash value and would give you "something back." The premium for this policy is $300 per year—three times as much as for the "non-permanent" plan.

The idea of getting something back really appeals to you, so you sign up for the higher cost program and start visualizing what you will do with all that promised money. The years go by and you go blissfully on your way. You pay the extra $200 each year and the insurance company sends you notices of your cash value increases and what a tremendous money-maker this policy is. (It's a money-maker all right—but not for you.)

At about the same time that your policy has a cash value of $1,000, your home catches fire. The damage amounts to $3,000. You notify the company of your loss and soon thereafter receive two checks—one for $2,000 and one for $1,000. The $1,000 check is identified as your cash value; the $2,000 check is identified as insurance company money.

At first you don't quite understand what's going on, but the company very blandly explains how this combination of protection and savings works. It's really very simple—when you have a loss, your cash value is used to pay a part of the claim. You weren't advised of this when you were sold the policy, but this is still the way it works.

It now becomes clear to you that the $100-per-year policy would have covered your fire loss just as completely as the $300-per-year plan; that your selfish desire to get "something back" tripled your cost of protection for several years; that the $1,000 cash value which you had thought was yours actually paid the insurance company's debt; that you actually had a policy with a $1,000 "deductible," but didn't even know about it.

NOTE: You don't need to start examining your fire insurance policy for its cash value. Fire insurance companies sell protection only—not this silly combination of protection and savings. These companies realize that you would refuse to buy such a ridiculous idea. However, you should start checking your permanent life insurance policies (including any that might be paid up) and see how much of a "deductible" you are carrying. *You might be carrying more of the risk than the company which is charging you premiums.*

So that you won't have to turn back to the previous diagram, here is a picture of a typical whole-life policy issued at age 35. You will note that each increase in cash value produces a higher "deductible" for you. At age 65, your "deductible" would be 52.2% of the face amount.

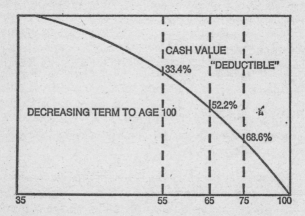

IF PERMANENT INSURANCE IS SUCH A POOR BUY, WHY DO MOST SALESMEN RECOMMEND THIS TYPE?

Greed and ignorance of both buyer and seller. You like the idea of getting "something back" and you aren't as knowledgeable about life insurance as you need to be.

The salesman likes the higher commissions of permanent insurance and his company trains him to sell this type because this is where the money is—for them! Also, many salesmen don't really understand what they are selling, and they are completely convinced that permanent insurance is the answer to everything and the only type you should consider. These salesmen have been so brainwashed that it is practically impossible for some of them to admit that term insurance even exists. They continue to parrot the overworked slogans and sales pitches that have been pumped into them at countless sales meetings. When they sell you a $5,000 whole-life policy instead of $30,000-$40,000 of honest protection term insurance, they sincerely and wholeheartedly believe they are doing you a tremendous favor.

NOTE: Wouldn't it be an interesting development if an agent delivering a check to a widow were required to explain why he sold her husband a $5,000 whole-life policy when the same amount of premium would have provided $30,000 of real death protection? Or perhaps it would be better if the insurance company were required to put the explanation in writing and then accept the liability for the difference in death benefits. Don't expect anything like this to happen in the foreseeable future. It is a rather interesting thought, however.

BUT I'VE BEEN TOLD THAT PEOPLE WON'T SAVE UNLESS FORCED TO DO SO AND THAT FORCED SAVING PERMANENT INSURANCE IS THE IDEAL WAY TO DO IT.

This is more brainwashing by the life insurance industry. To quote Ralph Nader:

> "For almost seventy years the life insurance industry has been a smug sacred cow feeding the public a steady line of sacred bull."*

It's true that many people don't save for the future. However, there are just as many who do. Otherwise, there wouldn't be the billions of dollars in savings accounts, bonds, stocks, mutual funds, real estate and other investments. Who forces these people to save?

If permanent life insurance is such a wonderful road to financial security, why are so many senior citizens dependent upon friends, welfare and charity for their

*From statements during the 1973 Congressional investigation of pricing practices of the life insurance industry.

daily existence? The first American life insurance company was established over two-hundred years ago, in 1759. The industry has become richer and richer over the years, while the plight of our elderly has worsened. It seems that if permanent insurance was as good as its advocates claim, then all retirees should be living in the lap of luxury. As you know, this is not the case.

Cash value insurance is so heavily "front-loaded" that the savings account takes forever to get off the ground. When 80% or more of your first-year whole-life premium is used for company expenses and the cash value only earns 2½% to 3½% per year, it's almost impossible to accumulate any worthwhile amount of money in a permanent insurance policy. Even endowment plans, which stress the savings idea more than whole life, provide a very small profit to the buyer.

The greatest objection to permanent insurance as a savings device (and one that the life insurance industry is finally—but grudgingly—admitting) is that it provides no hedge against inflation. When the cost of living is increasing at 9% or more per year and the cash value is poking along at 2½% to 3½%, the gap between the two becomes wider and wider. Even if your *entire* premium earned this 2% or 3%, it would be inadequate. With only a *portion* of your premium credited to the cash value (remember the "front-loading"), the true growth rate is even less adequate.

To illustrate, let's assume you are age 35 and are able to save $1000 per year until age 65. Your prime objective is retirement income and you are not concerned about death benefits.

Your friendly life insurance salesman tells you that if you put this $1000 per year into a non-par whole life policy, you will get all your money back at age 65. For your $1000 per year for 30 years, his company will guarantee that you will have $34,224 at age 65 or $4,224 more than you put in. The death benefit would be $69,000 in case you didn't make it to age 65.

In comparison, here are the values at age 65 of $1000 per year invested at various rates of interest:

Interest Rate	Value at age 65
3%	$ 49,000
4%	58,328
5%	69,760
6%	83,802
8%	122,346
10%	180,943

Any questions as to why cash value life insurance is a poor investment?

BUT THE SALESMAN SHOWED ME WHERE MY DIVIDENDS WOULD GROW OVER THE YEARS AND MORE THAN KEEP UP WITH INFLATION.

Did he also tell you how much you were being overcharged so that you would receive dividends? The average is about 30% overcharge for a par policy versus a nonpar of the same type.

Did he imply that dividends were certain and guaranteed? All dividend illustrations are supposed to include a statement reading something like this:

"Dividends illustrated are based on our current scale—not a guarantee, estimate or promise of dividend results."

This hedge clause (quite often in fine print) relieves the company of any responsibility when actual dividends are less than illustrated dividends. With no obligation to fulfill their guesstimates, a company can illustrate almost any amounts it chooses. By showing you a dividend illustration, a salesman can present quite a fantastic picture of life insurance as an investment.

Salesmen, many times using company-prepared forms, have been known to combine the future cash values of a policy, which are guaranteed, with the illustrated dividends, which are not guaranteed. The implication is that this combination of cash value and dividends is an absolute and certain result. 'Tain't so!

Another technique a company uses is to set premiums much higher than really needed—in other words, an extra overcharge on top of the first overcharge. The total premium therefore is huge enough (with your money) so that the company can easily pay seemingly generous dividends. It can then "point with pride" to its wonderful record. Just remember that *you* are supplying this extra money and at no charge to the company.

BUT I'VE BEEN TOLD THAT THE COMPANIES INVEST THIS MONEY AND PAY OUT THE PROFITS TO THE POLICYHOLDERS.

This is more of the "sacred bull" mentioned by Mr. Nader. The companies do invest your money—what they don't spend on themselves and their salesmen. And the life insurance industry certainly does have some pretty fine investments. But don't bet that you are getting your share of the profits. An insurance company has many ways of spending your money that do not benefit you. This is especially true of the mutual companies with no stockholders to worry about. However, don't conclude that stock life companies are necessarily penny pinchers, either. Both types pay out a good hunk of your dollars for commissions, plush offices, sales conventions, and other "amenities."

The income tax treatment of insurance policy dividends is the real clue. If these payments were truly profits (as are dividends from common stocks), you can be sure that the Internal Revenue Service would require you to pay income tax on them. Since they are partial refunds of a previous overcharge, the IRS recognizes that they are not taxable income to you.

IF MY DIVIDENDS AREN'T TAXABLE, WHY DID MY INSURANCE COMPANY SEND ME A YEAR-END TAX STATEMENT?

That's a different matter. You have a choice of taking dividends in cash, using them to pay premiums, of buying additional paid-up insurance, or letting them accumulate at interest. If you leave them with the company at interest, you are taxed on this interest the same as if the money were in a savings account.

The interest rate on accumulated dividends paid by most life insurance companies is usually less than you can obtain from a credit union or savings and loan association. If you have been leaving your dividends with the insurance company, you would do better to withdraw them, put the money in a savings account, and take future dividends in cash.

NOTE: You would do even better if you bought new term insurance, canceled your dividend-paying policy and put the accumulated dividends, cash value, and savings in premium into a savings account.

Many buyers are confused and do not understand the difference between cash value and dividends. The salesman may cite an accumulation rate of 4% or 5% for dividends and thus imply that you are getting this rate on both cash value and dividends. This diagram may clarify the situation:

Accumulated dividends

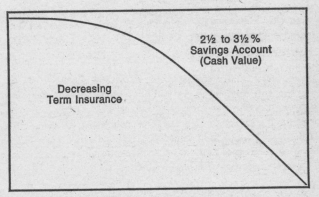

2½ to 3½%
Savings Account
(Cash Value)

Decreasing
Term Insurance

Typical cash value policy (participating)

The cash value builds up *within* the policy and does not increase the death benefit in anyway. It only reduces your actual protection at exactly the same rate as the cash value increases.

Insurance policy dividends are *external* features of participating policies that result from an intentional overcharge cranked into the premium. If you leave these dividends with the insurance company, you receive interest on the amount accumulated. The rate of interest varies from time to time and from company to company. It is not a fixed, guaranteed rate as is the cash value rate. The confusion (and possibly misrepresentation) results when you are told that the company's current accumulation rate is 5% (for example) and then conclude that you are getting 5% on all your money. So don't swallow any such statement. OK?

BUT MY CASH VALUE INCREASES TAX-FREE. IF I PUT THIS MONEY INTO A SAVINGS ACCOUNT, IT BECOMES TAXABLE.

Did you ever stop to ask why you are not taxed on increases in cash value? Here's why. Every time the cash value increases, your true protection decreases and the company has less of the total risk. Is there any good reason for you to be taxed on something that benefits someone else?

NOTE: You can put the money into Series E bonds with no current income taxes. Or you can buy tax-exempt securities.

The companies love to tell you that permanent insurance is the most wonderful tax-sheltered device ever invented and send you pretty statements each year showing you how your dividends and cash value increases have reduced your cost of insurance. However, you are not told that your actual protection reduces each year, nor that your cost of protection increases each year. Instead, they obscure the true picture with misleading and deceptive statements to keep you overpaying for your insurance.

BUT I WAS TOLD THAT I WOULD GET ALL MY MONEY BACK AT AGE 65 AND THAT MY INSURANCE WOULD HAVE COST ME NOTHING.

This is all part of their technique to get more money from you by promising you "something back." The outmoded and now discredited Net Cost Method supported this sales pitch. The Interest-Adjusted Method isn't the greatest system ever devised, but it's much more honest than the Net Cost Method. You will recall that the IAM showed a *cost* to the policyholder. Don't be so naïve as to believe that you will get anything for free from a life insurance company.

IS PERMANENT INSURANCE EVER USEFUL OR DESIRABLE?

Permanent insurance can be useful in some specialized cases. For instance, if you accumulate an estate larger than $120,000, there would be federal and state estate taxes to be paid. This would require ready cash. If your estate was made up of assets not easily convertible into cash (real estate, closely held company stock that is not publicly traded, uncollectible accounts, unmarketable securities) permanent insurance would be a way of providing the ready cash needed for estate taxes. "Estate liquidity" is the phrase normally used to identify this need and it is an important consideration.

The cash-value advocates would like to have you believe that permanent insurance is the one and only way to provide this requirement. However, if your holdings are made up of "liquid" assets such as listed securities, mutual funds, savings accounts, certificates of deposit and similar marketable assets, you would have little or no need for permanent life insurance. Your heirs would simply sell whatever was needed to pay the estate taxes.

NOTE: Life insurance proceeds may be excluded from your taxable estate if you are not the owner of the insurance at time of your death. You should consider making your wife the owner of your policies for this reason. Check this out with your attorney or the trust department of your bank. Do not go only by the salesman's "advice."

Another situation justifying permanent insurance might be the desire to leave a specific amount of money to your church, school, or favorite charity. Life insurance is a simple way to accomplish this objective. You just buy the desired amount of insurance and name the organization of your choice as the beneficiary. You get an income tax deduction for the premiums during your lifetime, and when you die the proceeds are paid directly to the beneficiary with little or no delay.

Just because you might become wealthy enough to have to be concerned about estate taxes at your death is no reason for you to buy permanent insurance now. The only consideration you now have is your future ability to buy insurance if you should become rich. (You may not be very rich if you give too much money to an insurance company!) You can guarantee your future eligibility for permanent insurance with renewable and convertible term that is convertible without proof of insurability up to age 65.

To illustrate, let's say you are now age 35 and decide to buy whole life at $17.55 per $1,000. At age 65 the cash value of this policy would be $522. Here are the figures:

Face value	$1,000.00
Cash value	−$ 522.00 (52.2%)
Actual protection	$ 478.00
Annual premium	$ 17.55 (age 35)
Plus 5% of cash value	$ 26.10
Actual cost	$ 43.65
Cost per $1,000 of protection	$ 91.32*

At age 65 you can buy a brand-new whole-life policy for $70.10 per $1,000—$21.22 less than the cost of protection in the whole-life policy bought at age 35. As long as your term insurance is convertible up to age 65, you will be money ahead to buy term now and convert later—if you need to. Even though the *premium* at age 65 will be higher than at age 35, the cost per $1,000 of protection is substantially less. Also, you will be paying this premium for a smaller number of years, and if you are wealthy enough to have estate tax problems or to make bequests, you certainly should be able to afford the higher premium. There really is no advantage in buying permanent insurance when you are young, is there?

NOTE: The average family (to whom this book is primarily directed) does not have estate tax problems. However, the survivors could very well have very serious financial problems if Dad is sold an inadequate amount of permanent insurance instead of an adequate amount of pure protection term insurance. If he is conned into buying the wrong type of insurance because he is promised

*($43.65 divided by .478)

"something back," his widow and children may well end up paying for his bad decision.

Can you visualize a picture of a jackass on a treadmill vainly trying to reach a carrot dangling in front of him? Unfortunately, this is very descriptive of the plight of too many husbands and fathers who have been persuaded to buy permanent insurance because they might get the "carrot" of cash value and dividends. Many of these men will die, still entranced with the idea of getting "something back," and will never realize how much they are overpaying for protection nor how badly they are underprotecting their families.

Are *you* on this treadmill?

CHAPTER SIX

ALL THAT GLITTERS IS NOT GOLD

It's no secret that the life insurance companies have very brainy and persuasive people to design and sell their products. Their expertise and razzle-dazzle selling techniques are aimed toward the uninformed buyers, and admittedly the industry has done a superb job of confusing and misleading the public.

The most common sales pitch is to emphasize what you (the buyer) will get back. This basic emphasis on cash values and dividends has been further amplified by adding other "goodies" designed to separate you from your money and to overpay for protection. You may be shown how you can have an income tax deduction with a certain plan, or how you can receive "guaranteed endowments" or some other feature that camouflages the true purpose of life insurance and creates unnecessary expenditure and confusion to you.

MODIFIED LIFE INSURANCE

A form of life insurance that you may come across is "mod," which is short for "modified." This is used in at least two different ways to describe life insurance plans. Here are some illustrations:

"Mod 3 Whole Life": This title is used to designate a permanent plan of life insurance with low premiums for the first three years and higher premiums thereafter. This is a favorite of the mutual companies, and is no bargain. It is simply a device to suck you into the wrong type of life insurance by baiting you with a low beginning premium. It may be a "Mod 5" or some other number of 10 or less.

A second form of the "mod" designation is shown in

"Mod 65" or "Mod 70." An alternate title might be "Double Protection to Age 65." The translation is that the face amount is reduced by one-half at age 65 or 70. In other words, it is a policy consisting of one-half whole life and one-half level term to age 65 or 70.

The premiums for plans such as these are usually less than for whole life, and if you feel you must have life insurance beyond age 65 or 70, you would be better off with a "Mod 65" or a "Mod 70" policy than with regular whole life.

NOTE: Don't overlook the availability of term plans that may be continued to age 100. You can buy a separate decreasing-term-to-age-100 policy or you might select the deposit term plan mentioned earlier. This may be converted to decreasing term to age 100 at the end of any ten-year level term period, even after age 65.

MINIMUM DEPOSIT INSURANCE

This is usually an overpriced whole-life or life-paid-up-at-age-65 policy specially fabricated for the "minimum deposit" selling technique. The mutual companies are the leading advocates of minimum deposit, but many stock companies push this idea also. It is frequently a participating policy.

The premium is artificially high in order to create a substantial first-year cash value. In addition to the normal overcharge for dividends and cash value, an extra amount is cranked into the premiums, with the excess being credited to the cash value. It is your money that produces this attractive first-year cash value (normally about 70% of the gross premium), not the benevolence of the insurance company.

This high first-year cash value enables you to borrow against the policy to pay the premium. For instance, the annual premium for a typical minimum deposit plan for age 35 would be about $23.00 per $1,000. The first-year cash value would be about $17.00 per $1,000. Instead of you paying the entire $23.00 in cash, you would be encouraged to borrow the $17.00 at 6% interest and pay only the $6.00 per $1,000 difference in cash.

NOTE: At age 35, you can buy five-year renewable and convertible term for $3.09 per $1,000. If you bought the minimum deposit idea, you would be paying $6.00 plus interest on $17.00, a total of $7.03. This is 2.27 times as much as the term premium.

The loan of $17.00 would be deducted from the face amount in case of your death. To offset this reduction, the minimum deposit plans include a "fifth-dividend option" which means that your dividend is used to buy one-year term insurance equal to the amount of your loan.

If the plan is a non-participating policy, it may include a feature known as "return of cash value." This is another swindle to make you think you are getting a bargain. Instead of the customary overcharge for dividends, the premium includes an overcharge to offset your borrowed cash value. Ingenious, isn't it?

In the following years, you continue to borrow the annual increase in cash value and pay the interest on the cumulative loan. Since interest costs are deductible from income, you are shown how you can reduce your taxable income and get practically free life insurance. Sounds like what you have always been looking for? Don't be too sure!

The amount of your loan increases each year that you borrow to pay the inflated premium. The interest costs also increase and end up being higher than for pure protection term insurance. Since you are borrowing all or most of your cash value plus using the dividends, you end up with little or no surrender value—just a huge annual interest cost.

The interest must be paid in cash (not borrowed from the insurance company) in order to be deducted from your income. If you don't have the money to pay the interest, you certainly cannot afford to pay off the loan, so you probably would be forced to drop the policy and lose the remaining protection. If you are no longer insurable because of poor health, you are in deep trouble. *In reality, it's your family that's in trouble.*

Minimum deposit insurance is simply a scheme to produce more commission for the salesman since he receives a higher rate for selling permanent plans than for term. All the cash value and dividends are milked out of the policy and you end up with nothing—no protection, no cash value, no dividends, no salvage value. Just a bunch of interest costs.

NOTE: In the early years of minimum deposit, all interest costs were fully deductible. The Internal Revenue Service now requires that a policy be in force for at least three years before you can deduct interest for a policy loan. The IRS determined that minimum deposit plans were artificial contrivances designed to sell overpriced insurance. There may be even further IRS restrictions in the future.

A twist on the minimum deposit idea is to offer you the services of a friendly lending institution (frequently associated with the life company) that will loan you the money to pay the premium for permanent insurance. The proposal for this "financed insurance" shows how you can first borrow from the loan company, and then later use your accumulated cash value to pay off the first loan, thereby trading off one loan for another. The only ones who benefit from such an arrangement are the salesman, the insurance company and the "Friendly Finance Company"—all at your expense.

Another variation of the minimum deposit idea is to "integrate" your present policies with new insurance. Here the pitch is to show you how you can buy additional insurance without increasing your premium outlay, and get tax deductions as well.

By borrowing against your present policies to pay the premiums for both new and old insurance, you avoid higher out-of-pocket costs. If your old policies are at least three years old, the interest on these loans will probably be deductible from your income. So you save income taxes and get more insurance at no extra cost. It looks like a real bonanza, doesn't it?

If you fall for all this razzle-dazzle and fancy figurework, you will be doing nothing but depleting the cash values of your old policies and creating an ever larger debt and annual interest charge. You would be much better off to buy new term insurance and then cash in the old policies. You would then have honest protection at a lower cost per $1,000. Instead of your paying 5% or 6% to use your own money, your cash values could be earning interest for you. Wouldn't this be much better?

PROFIT-SHARING POLICIES

Another type of plan to avoid like the plague is the one that offers you the glitter of sharing in company profits. These may be called "Founder's Plan," "Charter Policy," "President's Plan," "Capital Growth Plan" or some other equally high-sounding title contrived to whet your appetite. They are all overpriced life insurance plans camouflaged as investment programs.

The basic policy is usually twenty-payment life, although some companies use whole life. The typical plan includes the customary bait of cash value and dividends plus such items as "guaranteed annual endowments," return of premium in case of death during the premium paying period, additional monthly income in case of death, and other similar features. The big bait, however, is that *you* are a chosen person; only a limited number of such plans are being sold and therefore only a few, selected persons will have the opportunity to share in the profits of this tremendous company. Have you heard this pitch?

These are favorite devices of new life insurance companies. By showing the fantastic profits of the older companies, they imply that this brand-new company will also be a money-maker. The plans have astronomical premiums to produce high commissions for the professional hucksters who are hired to peddle all these "goodies." Frequent targets are parents and grandparents who are persuaded to buy them for their children and grandchildren. If you buy a program, you may be appointed to the company's "Board of Reference"—so that you can refer your friends to the salesman who sold you this unbelievable way to untold riches.

NOTE: Several states have either outlawed or drastically curtailed the sale of founder and charter policies. If you are offered one—don't buy it. If you have one—get rid of it. If you feel that you have been taken advantage of, advise your state insurance department of the circumstances.

VARIABLE LIFE INSURANCE

The claims of the permanent insurance advocates that cash-value life insurance is a tremendous investment are beginning to be questioned by both buyers and the companies themselves. It has become more and more obvious that the fixed dollars of permanent life insurance provide no hedge against inflation. Because of this awareness, several life insurance companies have started selling mutual funds and other equity-type investments. The stock market hasn't been very cooperative during a large part of this period, and the life insurance salesmen dislike the low commissions paid for selling mutual funds. An alternate approach now being considered by some companies is variable life insurance.

The idea of variable life insurance is to provide a death benefit and a cash surrender value that will increase with the cost of living. Instead of a fixed, guaranteed amount, both the death benefit and the cash surrender value would depend upon the value of an investment in stocks, bonds and other securities. As the market value of the separate investment increased, so would these other values. If an investment value decreased, so would the death and surrender values, but only to a definite and predetermined amount. They would not drop to zero.

Variable life involves the sale of securities which is governed by much tighter regulations (both state and federal) than is the sale of life insurance. For example, the mutual fund salesman must give you a detailed prospectus which spells out the sales charge and other costs. This "full disclosure" aspect of securities sales isn't exactly palatable to the life insurance industry, and the companies interested in selling variable life insurance are doing their best to circumvent the laws and regulations that the mutual fund industry has to live with. This will take time, so don't expect to see very many companies selling variable life in the near future.

Actually, you can establish your own variable life plan very easily. You can buy level term life insurance to provide a constant and definite death benefit. You can then split the rest of your money into fixed and variable investments. For example, you could put 25% of your investment money into Series E government bonds. These are guaranteed, and you pay no income tax on the interest until you cash them in. The remaining 75% could go into a growth-type mutual fund or stocks of your own choosing. If you died your family would receive the guaranteed proceeds of the level term, plus the government bonds, plus the variable investment. If you didn't die, you would have the bonds and the investment for retirement income, but you would not have to drop your life insurance protection in order to use these assets. Neither would you have to pay interest for the use of your cash value if you didn't want to cancel your life insurance.

You would probably cancel or reduce the amount of life insurance when you retired, but you would not be forced to do so. The deposit term plan discussed earlier may be continued to age 100, if you so desire. If you believe you will want insurance after age 65 or 70, you should consider the idea of a deposit term plan plus separate fixed and variable investments. This combination would give you a variable life insurance plan.

SPLIT LIFE INSURANCE

Another new product of the life insurance industry that is being greeted with varying reactions is "Split Life." This is a fairly sound idea because it separates the savings element from the protection whereas the traditional permanent insurance combines the two elements into a single policy. Split life is two individual contracts:

1. A yearly renewable term life insurance policy
2. A retirement annuity

The annuity is comparable to the cash-value feature of permanent insurance, but since it is separated from the death benefit, a split life policy provides that in case of your death, your family receives the proceeds of the term insurance plus the value of the annuity.

Split life is a radical departure from permanent insurance and is heartily disliked by most insurance companies and salesmen. The main reason for this opposition is that you are told how inexpensively you can buy pure protection term insurance. This is heresy; better that the buyer be kept in the dark. Here are some sample annual premiums per $1,000 for split life yearly renewable level term compared with typical whole-life premiums:

Age	Split Life Term Premium	Typical Whole-Life Premium
25	$ 1.53	$12.17
30	1.91	14.53
35	2.30	17.54
40	3.12	21.35
45	4.68	26.20
50	7.56	32.00
55	12.05	40.64
60	19.15	52.25

However, before you decide that split life is the way to go, let's take a closer look. There's a snag that you need to be aware of.

In order to get the low-cost term insurance, you must first buy the annuity. For each $100 of annual annuity premium, you are permitted to buy $10,000 of term life insurance. You can buy the annuity without buying the term, but you cannot buy the split life term only. In other words, it's "invest and buy term," not "buy term and invest."

Most annuities are notoriously unproductive savings plans, and the split life annuities are no exception. They are highly "front-loaded," the same as permanent life insurance and as a result take about ten years before they equal what you have paid in. Here are the cash surrender values per $100 of annual premium for a split life annuity:

End of Year	Total Paid for Annuity	Cash Surrender Value
1	$ 100	$ 10 (90% 1st-year sales charge)
2	200	94
3	300	194
4	400	298
5	500	406
6	600	517
7	700	633
8	800	752
9	900	876
10	1,000	1,004

At the end of ten years, you would have a grand profit of $4 on an investment of $1,000.

Split life isn't the worst plan ever devised, but neither is it the best. You can adopt this idea without being clobbered with a 90% first-year sales charge that severely reduces the productivity of your money. Simply buy the term life insurance from a company that doesn't require you to also buy a miserable annuity. Then save your money independently. Series E government bonds aren't the most lucrative investments that you can make, but you must admit they are much better than an annuity that takes ten years to show a profit.

NOTE: These are just some of the plans offered by the life insurance industry. You can bet they will continue to devise schemes to get you to overpay for protection. Keep your guard up and don't let yourself be dazzled by "fool's gold."

CHAPTER SEVEN

FAMILY INSURANCE

Do you have life insurance on your children? WHY?
Do you have life insurance on your wife? WHY NOT?

If you ever need an illustration of upside-down priorities, you can find it in the life insurance program of the average American family. Here is what you will find in more cases than not:

1. Too little insurance on the husband and father.
2. Too much insurance on the children.
3. Practically no life insurance on the wife and mother.

Millions of parents have been sold permanent insurance for their children's education instead of adequate insurance on the husband and father. When the salesman cannot persuade you to buy his overpriced permanent insurance on your life, he will switch his pitch to money for Johnny's college and try to convince you to waste money for endowment plans and twenty-payment life policies on your children.

Endowments and limited-payment life plans are a bad buy at any time. They are tremendously overpriced and can easily qualify as one of the world's worst methods of accumulating money for future needs. College costs have skyrocketed even more than the cost of living, and there is simply no way that you can logically expect to meet these rising costs with a savings account earning 3½% or less. It's a rude awakening after years of paying premiums to find that the surrender value of that wonderful guaranteed savings policy is barely enough to pay the tuition for one semester of college!

NOTE: It's more than a rude awakening—it's a catastrophe when the father dies after having been sold insurance on his children instead of honest death protection on his own life.

Another example of upside-down priorities results from the asinine sales pitch: "Buy insurance while you are young when premiums are low." When you can't be persuaded to buy more insurance on your own life, the salesman then suggests that you give your children a head start on their insurance program, and proceeds to load you down with the highest-premium policies in his portfolio. Has this happened to you?

The economic value of a child is practically zero. Unless you have a child prodigy who is producing an income, you have an expense, not an asset. It costs much less to bury a youngster than to feed, clothe and educate him until he is a productive member of society. All the money in the world cannot compensate for the emotional loss resulting from the death of your son or daughter. Financially, however, you are money ahead, because you would no longer have the expense of raising your child to adulthood. This may sound hardhearted and callous, but it's true. And I would like to mention once again that there are other ways of saving money for your child's education —ways that will bring in bigger returns than endowment and limited life payment plans!

Consider also the question of who is going to pay the premiums for insurance on your children after your death, especially if you have insufficient insurance on your life. If your survivors don't have enough money to buy necessities, the policy on Junior will have to be lapsed or surrendered for a fraction of the amount paid in premiums.

Most insurance companies offer a "child insurance rider" that may be tacked onto a policy on your life, including term policies. These riders usually provide $1,000 of level term insurance to your child's age 21, 23 or 25 for a premium of less than $10 per year. One rider and one premium covers all children who are at least 15 days old and who are under age 18 when your policy is issued. Children born after the policy is issued are automatically covered once they are 15 days old. The premium is not increased at that time. A child insurance rider on your policy is a low cost way of providing ready cash for final expenses if a child dies, and it is recommended that you consider such a plan.

A feature of most child insurance riders is that at the end of the level term coverage (age 21 to 25), your off-spring is guaranteed that he can buy an individual policy, regardless of his physical condition. He is required to buy permanent insurance, but a standard premium whole life (from a stock company) would be better than no insurance at all. However, keep in mind that very few young adults are uninsurable and are able to buy all the insurance they need. *Just be sure your youngsters know that they should buy term!*

In summary, don't buy insurance on your children until you have adequate insurance on yourself. You are the breadwinner, and your death would be a much greater financial loss to your family than the death of a child.

NOTE: If you are not insurable, ask the salesman for a term policy on your wife with a child insurance rider.

WHAT ABOUT INSURANCE ON MY WIFE?

This is practically a necessity if you have children who are minors. Your wife is a cook, nursemaid, dietician, food buyer, dishwasher, housekeeper, laundress, seamstress, practical nurse, and chauffeur, to list a few of the services she provides. It's been estimated that hiring competent replacements would cost about $175 per week—$9,100 per year. This does not include the cost of replacing her companionship nor the higher income taxes you would pay as a widower.

If you have a working wife who is providing a part of the family income, her death would make an even greater dent in your financial situation.

This is not "women's lib" philosophy. It's cold, hard facts. If you have ever gone through an extended period of running a house and family while your wife was sick or absent, you can well appreciate these words. If you haven't had such an experience, give your wife a long vacation by herself, leaving the children in your care.

You can buy insurance on your wife by adding a "wife

insurance rider" to a term policy on your life, or by purchasing an individual term policy on her life. Stay away from the so-called "Family Policy" that is a combination of permanent insurance on your life, a lesser amount of permanent insurance on your wife and term insurance on your children. Here is an example of a family policy peddled by a major mutual life insurance company (husband age 30, wife age 25).

The basic policy on your life is "Modified Life Paid Up at Age 65" in the amount of $5,000. Your wife's coverage is $1,250 of life paid up at age 65. The children's coverage is $1,000 of level term to age 25. The premium is $136.90 per year for the first five years and $151.35 per year after the fifth year.

In comparison, this same annual premium of $136.90 will buy the following coverage from a major stock life insurance company:

$30,000 of decreasing term to age 65 on you.

$ 9,385 of 18-year decreasing term on your wife*

$ 1,000 of level term to age 25 on all your children

Alternately, if you decided to use the entire $136.90 for insurance on yourself only, you could buy $39,000 of honest family protection. You wouldn't receive any of those super dividends or cash values, but your family would have quite a few more dollars for bills in case of your death. If you were this thirty-year-old, how would you use this money?

MY PRESENT POLICIES ARE SET UP TO PAY MY WIFE A FIXED INCOME FOR LIFE. IS THIS A GOOD ARRANGEMENT?

NO! Your policies should authorize payment of the death proceeds in a lump sum. This is the only practical settlement option. The companies would like to have the money left with them to dole out on *their* terms, but don't go along with such an arrangement.

The life insurance industry is not noted for its generosity in spite of all the money spent on image building. Its

*After 18 years, the wife rider levels off at $1,000 until your age 65.

76

selfishness is especially evident when you examine the settlement options other than lump sum.

The most common income settlement is designated "ten-year certain and life," meaning that your widow would be guaranteed an income for as long as she lived. If she were to die within ten years after the first payment started, the unpaid amount would go to her beneficiary. Here is a typical ten-year certain settlement option for different ages:

Widow's Age	Monthly Income per $1,000
30	$2.78
35	2.97
40	3.20
45	3.47
50	3.81
55	4.23
60	4.73
65	5.34

To illustrate, if your widow were age 30 and you had a $10,000 policy, she would receive a guaranteed lifetime income of $27.80 per month. In ten years she would receive only $3,336. If she were to die soon after that, the company would have fulfilled its obligation and would keep the balance of the $10,000.

By comparison, your widow could put the $10,000 in a 6% savings account where it would earn $600 per year in interest—an average of $50 per month—without touching the $10,000.

A second reason against a lifetime income option is that such a choice could be very unfair to your widow. No matter how good a financial planner you may be, you cannot possibly forsee all the requirements your widow might have. If you restrict her to a set income for a given period of time or for her lifetime, you could very well be doing her a serious injustice. Once she starts receiving this "income she can't outlive," the balance of the money is tied up and she is limited to this same inflexible amount, regardless of how living costs increase. Is this what you want to inflict on your widow?

NOTE: If you question your widow's ability to handle a lump sum of money or are reluctant to support a second husband, the answer is a life insurance trust. Very briefly, this is a legal arrangement whereby you designate a trustee to receive the proceeds of your life insurance policies and to disburse this money as you direct. You will need an attorney to prepare this document and it is not recommended that you try doing it yourself. If you don't have an attorney, check with the trust department of your bank for their suggestions.

While on the subject of family insurance, you might see if you still have any small policies of $1,000 or less around the house. These are probably "industrial" or "nickel-a-week" "burial insurance" polices sold by "debit agents," who personally collect the premiums each week or month.

These types of insurance are tremendously costly. The most widely sold plans are twenty-payment life and twenty-year endowments of $1,000 or less. They are usually participating policies with a substantial overcharge for dividends. The premiums also include another overcharge to compensate for the salesman's time and travel expenses.

It's amazing how many people who should really know better have policies such as these lying around the house —policies that their parents bought for them twenty or thirty years ago.

Recommendation: If you have any of these antiques, don't worry about their historical value. Just cash them in without delay. There is so little actual protection in them that they just aren't worth keeping.

CHAPTER EIGHT

OTHER FORMS OF LIFE INSURANCE

Most of the life insurance in force today is individual coverage bought from a salesman. However, there are other forms of life insurance that need to be considered.

GROUP LIFE INSURANCE

The most common form of nonindividual insurance is group life insurance. This is usually term insurance, and your employer often pays all or part of the premiums. It is frequently combined with hospital and medical coverage. The premiums for group life insurance are less than for individual policies, and you therefore get more protection per dollar of premium than you can buy on your own.

The main advantage of group life is its low cost. Even if you are paying the entire premium yourself with no help from your employer, the cost of protection is very easy on your budget. But group life is not all roses.

A very serious weakness of most group plans is that you lose this low-cost protection if and when you leave your employer. Most group plans permit you to convert your coverage to individual insurance without evidence of insurability. However, it is required that you buy permanent insurance at a substantial increase in premium within thirty days following termination of employment. If you don't convert within this time, your protection ends. You may not want permanent insurance, but if you are uninsurable, you would have no choice.

If you were to change employment, your new employer might not have a group plan. If he did, the amount of coverage might be less than with your old employer. Also, there is frequently a waiting period before new employees become eligible for group plans. If your old coverage stops before you are eligible for the new plan, there would be an interval of reduced protection for your family.

If you leave your present job to go into business for yourself, you would also lose your group coverage. If you were to be laid off by your present employer, you probably could not afford to convert your group insurance to an individual permanent insurance plan.

These are some of the conditions that could make group life insurance a very indefinite and undependable part of your total insurance program. Rather than taking a chance on your family's not having this protection, you would be on safer ground to exclude your group insurance from your thinking. If it's available to you, take it, and then forget you have it. Buy all the individual term insurance your family needs just as if you had no group insurance.

NOTE: Some group plans accept you automatically without requiring proof of insurability. If you cannot qualify for individual insurance because of poor health and if your employer's plan accepts all comers, get the maximum amount. Even if you are forced to convert at a later date, the permanent insurance would usually be at standard rates. Not all group plans accept all employees, but many of them do.

SERVICEMEN'S GROUP LIFE INSURANCE (SGLI)

A specialized form of group insurance, SGLI, automatically provides coverage to all active duty military personnel. As with other group plans, it ends soon after you leave active duty and is convertible without evidence of insurability. This conversion option can be very valuable if you are disabled and cannot buy insurance at standard rates. If you are healthy when you leave military service, the conversion option is of no value because it requires that you buy permanent insurance.

This guaranteed conversion feature of SGLI is sometimes capitalized on by unscrupulous salesmen who are more interested in commissions than anything else. By implying that conversion is the only way for the newly discharged veteran to get life insurance, these vultures haunt the separation centers and load the new civilian down with high-cost permanent insurance. If you are now in military service or have sons and daughters in service, be aware of this miserable practice. To repeat, the only time the SGLI conversion option is valuable is if you are disabled and cannot buy individual insurance at standard rates.

In 1974, Congress established a new insurance plan for discharged servicemen called the Veterans Group Life Insurance (VGLI). This is a very low cost five year level term plan and a discharged serviceman can purchase up to $20,000 coverage for practically nothing. VGLI cannot be renewed after the five years, but may be converted to permanent insurance with a commercial company. Like SGLI, conversion is guaranteed, regardless of physical condition.

The same caution applies to VGLI as to SGLI. If you are insurable, buy term insurance; if not insurable, convert to non-par whole life. Also, be sure to do some shopping beforehand.

ASSOCIATION INSURANCE

Another form of "group type" insurance is "association insurance." True group requires that you be an employee; association insurance is based on membership in an organization or in a given profession. There are many such plans available to accountants, attorneys, engineers, physicians, military personnel, and others. The majority of them require that you continue to be a member of the organization or be active in the specific profession. Most are term insurance plans.

The rates for association term insurance are sometimes lower than for individual term insurance, but not always. Don't assume that just because an association plan offers rates that appear to be low when compared with permanent insurance, that it is the best you can do. Shop around before you decide.

A point to look for is how long you are guaranteed that you can keep the policy in force. Some plans provide that if you cease working as an accountant, for example, you lose your eligibility. Others are guaranteed renewable to age 65 or 70, regardless of how you earn your living. This is particularly true of several plans for active-duty military personnel. If you buy the policy while on active duty, you can keep it after you leave active duty, but do not have to convert to permanent insurance.

If an association insurance plan is sponsored by a well-established national organization, there is a reasonable chance that your coverage and premiums will continue as stated in the policy. However, there may be a hedge clause that allows the insurance company to raise premiums, reduce the amount of coverage or terminate the program completely. In this respect, association insurance has the same weakness as true group insurance. You will probably feel a lot safer with individual term insurance that only you can cancel.

INSURANCE BY MAIL

Mail-order life insurance may be a tremendous buy or a complete waste of your money. There is no law requiring you to purchase your life insurance from a salesman. You are completely free to buy how and where you decide. However, unless you are more knowledgeable about life insurance than most buyers, you can very easily be led astray by mail-order insurance.

If you are tempted by a mail-order offer, be certain that the company is registered and licensed in your state. The literature may say that it is, but to be sure, check with your state insurance department. If the company is not licensed, forget their offer because you would have no protection under your state laws.

Also beware of plans that guarantee to insure you regardless of your physical condition or without any question about your health. These plans are highly overpriced, and unless you are absolutely positive that you are uninsurable, stay away from them. The usual technique is to limit the death benefit to the amount of premium paid if you die within a given period of time, such as three years.

If you survive this trial period, you have the full coverage, but at a pretty stiff premium.

NOTE: Mail-order insurance is another example of how the life insurance industry takes advantage of the general public's ignorance about life insurance. Several states have clamped down on the companies that have circulated misleading and incomplete literature. Hopefully, this trend will continue.

CREDIT LIFE INSURANCE

When you finance the purchase of a car or other large item or borrow money for other purposes, you are usually offered "credit life." This is a form of decreasing term insurance that pays off the loan if you die before you have completed the payments. It's similar to mortgage insurance on your home loan, but at considerably higher premiums.

Rates vary by states and by loaning organizations, but a fairly representative premium is 75 cents per $100 of indebtedness. This figures out to $7.50 per $1,000 for two- or three-year decreasing term.

You are not required to buy credit life if you don't want it. The loan company is required to tell you how much it costs and to itemize the charge separate from interest and carrying charges. If you take time to analyze the cost, you will find that you are paying an inflated premium in more cases than not. You would do better to include some extra term insurance in your regular life insurance program to cover anticipated installment loans.

NOTE: One advantage of credit life is that you do not have to prove that you are insurable. If you cannot buy life insurance because of poor health, credit life may be a bargain.

VETERANS LIFE INSURANCE (NSLI)

If you served in the Armed Forces during World War II or the Korean War, you probably had National Service Life Insurance (NSLI). The active duty form of NSLI was five-year renewable and convertible level term that could be continued on the same basis after leaving active duty. If you made this choice, congratulate yourself for not converting to some form of permanent insurance that the Veterans Administration did and still does recommend.

If you were persuaded to convert your low-cost term insurance to whole-life or thirty-payment life by the VA propaganda, you may still be able to change your mind and get some of your money back. Contact your nearest VA Center and ask for the forms to convert to "Modified Life." This is a low-cost, level premium plan that is one-half level term to age 65 or 70, and one-half whole life. The face value drops 50% at either age 65 or 70, depending upon which plan you select.

You must be able to pass a physical exam to convert your higher premium plan to modified life. If your application is approved, your new policy is backdated to the age when you first converted the term coverage. Your new premium will be lower and you will also receive a refund of the difference in cash value between the new modified life policy and your present permanent NSLI policy.

Even if your present NSLI policy is paid up, it will be to your advantage to switch to modified life. You will quite likely find that the cash value of your present NSLI policy put to work at 5% will pay most of the premium for the modified life plan.

NOTE: If you are not insurable, you might consider borrowing your NSLI cash value and putting this money to work in other ways.

NOTE: If you now have an NSLI policy of any type, get it out and check the beneficiary payout option. Unless you have specifically authorized a lump sum settlement (Option 1), your beneficiary will be forced to accept some form of installment payment of the proceeds. The shortest possible payout period is thirty-six months, with monthly payments of $28.99 per $1,000 of face value. In a thirty-six-month period, the total amount paid out is $1,043.64. This is a very meager return, because the $1,000 paid in a lump sum will earn at least $50 per year in a 5% savings account and a total of $150 (without compounding) in a thirty-six-month period.

CHAPTER NINE

BUY TERM — INVEST THE DIFFERENCE

Up to this point, we have been mainly concerned with the value of pure protection term insurance as a source of money for your survivors in case you don't live long enough to earn this money yourself. We have pointed out how much more protection you can provide for your family with low-cost term insurance than with the over-priced permanent insurance. You have been warned about some of the many devious schemes and plans that the life insurance industry has developed to get your money. Hopefully, you will heed this advice and avoid being talked into cash value insurance simply because *you* might get "something back." The life insurance companies have some of the most persuasive and accomplished salesmen in the world. They can easily dazzle you with their figure-work and slick phrases to make you forget that the prime reason for life insurance is protection for your wife and children.

According to the 1958 mortality table, about 68% of our population is still alive at age 65. In other words, only 32% die before age 65. You don't know if you will be alive at age 65 or not, but the odds are in your favor that you will reach that age and live for many years thereafter.

At age 65, you will have a life expectancy of another fourteen or fifteen years, based on present statistics. This can be a tremendously long time if you are trying to pay your bills on the income from that "super" cash value life insurance policy.

Many husbands and fathers have been persuaded to buy permanent insurance because "it will be there when your family needs it, regardless of when you die." (Sound familiar?) In the very next breath, the salesman tells you: "And at age 65, you will have a guaranteed income of X dollars per month—an income that you can't outlive." What he doesn't bother to explain is that X dollars per month probably won't be enough. Neither will he mention that *the instant that you exchange your cash value for retirement income, you no longer have any life insurance.* The remaining protection (the difference between the face value and the cash value) ends just as completely and just as certainly as if you had bought term to age 65 in the beginning. There is simply no way for you to have both protection and your money when you put all your dollars into cash-value life insurance.

Your first concern should be adequate protection for your family. If this takes all your available cash with none left over to save for retirement, put your family's welfare ahead of everything else. Buy the necessary amount of term insurance, pat yourself on the back for being so considerate and unselfish, and enjoy the satisfaction of knowing that your widow and orphans will have a decent living if you aren't around to provide it. This isn't to say that you should forget your need for retirement income; it's simply a matter of putting first things first.

On the other hand, you may have enough income to pay the premiums for permanent insurance. This is still a poor reason for misusing your money in this manner. There are many better ways to accumulate money for the future than with cash value life insurance.

BUT THE CASH VALUES ARE GUARANTEED!

You are right! They *are* guaranteed—to cost you money. Cash-value life insurance and its 2½ to 3½% return has not kept pace with inflation. You may have been shown illustrations of all the dollars that you might have at age 65 if you bought this modern financial miracle. It's quite possible that the figures you were shown included nonguaranteed dividends along with the guaranteed cash value. You should realize by now that you should avoid dividend type policies (both term and permanent) and buy only non-par term insurance.

Getting back to the guarantees, keep in mind that the word "guarantee" means so much and no more. Permanent life insurance can guarantee you a specific number of dollars at retirement time, but there is no way that you can be guaranteed that this amount of dollars will be enough to pay the anticipated higher prices for food, clothing, shelter, medical care and other expenses that you might have. We have had inflation in varying degrees since time began. If you are betting that it will stop or even slow down appreciably, you are bucking some really rough odds. Even the life insurance industry is grudgingly admitting the deficiencies of cash values as a means of accumulating adequate retirement income. This is why so many life insurance companies are now selling mutual funds and variable annuities. Buyers are becoming more knowledgeable about money and are questioning the claims of the permanent insurance advocates.

If you insist on having a guarantee, you can have it. All you need to do is to buy term insurance and put the difference into Series E government bonds. This isn't the most productive way to save money, but it sure beats giving it to an insurance company to save for you. The government doesn't soak you with a 70%-80% first-year sales charge; the bonds can be expected to earn at least 5% per year, and you don't have to worry about the safety of your money. You can easily arrange to buy bonds through your employer or through your bank.

CAN YOU EXPLAIN HOW THIS COULD WORK?

Let's assume you are age 30 and need at least $50,000 of life insurance. Let's also agree that you realize you should not buy participating insurance and are debating between $50,000 of non-par whole life (annual premium $732.50) and $50,000 of non-par decreasing term to age 65 (annual premium $172.50).* The difference in pre-

---

*These figures are typical of what is offered; they are not taken from any one particular company. They are used here merely to illustrate a point.

muim is $560 per year for Series E government bonds. Here's the comparison:

	Whole Life	Term Plus 5% Bonds
Annual premium (age 30)	$ 732.50	$ 172.50
Annual difference	none	+ 560.00
Total per year	$ 732.50	$ 732.50
Total paid to age 65 (35x$732.50)	$25,637.50	$25,637.50
Cash surrender value at age 65	$27,750.00	None
Value of bonds at age 65	None	$53,110.00
Profit at age 65	$ 2,112.50	$27,472.50
Difference in results		$25,360.00 more

Which is the better way to use your money? Give it to the insurance company to invest for *its* future or invest it yourself for *your* future?

BUT WITH THE TERM PLAN, I WON'T HAVE ANY INSURANCE AFTER AGE 65

With $53,110 in bonds, why would you need insurance? Insurance is simply a substitute for money. Once you have the money, you don't need the insurance. Also, don't forget that if you surrender your whole-life policy for cash at age 65, you are just as completely out of insurance as with the term policy. You cannot have both your cash and your protection with permanent insurance. When you come right down to it, "permanent insurance" isn't really very permanent, is it?

BUT LOOK AT THE INCOME TAXES I WOULD HAVE TO PAY ON MY PROFIT OF $27,472.50!

That's a real problem, isn't it? More people should have such a problem instead of wondering what they are going to live on after retirement. Shall we take a closer look?

If you bought Series E government bonds with the money that you didn't give to the insurance company, you would pay no taxes on the accumulated interest until you cashed them. But let's suppose that you cashed all your bonds at one time and that you were in the 50% tax bracket at the time. Here are the results:

Value of bonds at age 65	$53,110	$53,110
Less cash invested		
(35 years @ $560/year)	− 19,600	
Taxable interest	$33,510	
Income tax at 50%		− 16,755
Net after taxes		$36,355

If you were to cash in the whole life policy at age 65, you would have to pay tax on your profit of $2,112.50. Again assuming a 50% tax bracket, you would have a net after taxes of $26,693.75 ($27,750 cash value minus $1,056.25 for income taxes). This is almost $10,000 less than the after tax results of the term-bond method.

NOTE: Cashing all your bonds at one time would be impractical. A better way would be to exchange your "E" bonds for "H" bonds. You would not have to pay taxes on the accumulated interest. You would just buy $53,110 of H bonds and start receiving the interest in cash from then on. Assuming a 5% yield, your H bonds would give you an income of $2,655.50 per year, or $221.29 per month, without reducing principal. When you needed extra money, you could cash in some of the H bonds.

WHAT HAPPENS IF I USE THE CASH VALUE OF THE WHOLE-LIFE POLICY TO BUY RETIREMENT INCOME FROM THE INSURANCE COMPANY?

This would be an "annuity settlement" and would tie up your money for the rest of your life once you started receiving payments. (Don't forget—your insurance protection would end at the exact same instant!) For discussion purposes, let's say you go this route.

In round figures, it should take about $1,500 to buy a lifetime income of $10 per month for you at age 65. The $27,750 of cash value would therefore buy a retirement income of *$185 per month*. ($27,750 divided by $1,500 equals $185). This would be guaranteed to last as long as you did.

The H bonds, you will recall, would give you *$221.29 per month* without invading your principal. Your widow and children would also inherit the bonds at your death. Under the annuity settlement, there would be little or no refund.

If you bought a "joint and survivor annuity" for you and your wife, both of you would have a lifetime income. However, it would be less than the $185 per month that the single annuity on you would provide.

BUT WHAT IF I WANTED A LIFETIME INCOME WITHOUT TAKING A CHANCE OF USING UP ALL MY BONDS?

You would be falling right into a trap! If you were to cash in all your bonds, pay taxes at the 50% rate and then use the after-tax net of $36,355 to buy an annuity, you would end up with a monthly income of $242.36. This is only $21.07 more per month than the H bond interest *alone* would provide. Would you want to tie up all your money for such a small difference?

No matter what you have been told, you simply cannot obtain decent investment results with permanent insurance. Neither can you expect to obtain a very generous income from money left with an insurance company. They set the ground rules, and you can bet that they will place their interests above yours. The only sound approach is to buy low-cost term insurance for protection and then save the difference in other ways.

NOTE: A 50% tax bracket at age 65 is probably illogical, but was used to emphasize that the supposed tax advantages of permanent insurance are highly overrated. With a lower tax bracket, the advantages of setting up your own investment program would be even greater.

WHAT IF I SHOULD DIE BEFORE AGE 65?

Then your family would receive both the insurance proceeds and the bonds as shown below:

End of Year	Your Age	Insurance Protection	Value of Bonds	Estate Value
5	35	$45,600	$ 3,248	$48,848
10	40	40,500	7,397	47,897
15	45	34,600	12,689	47,289
20	50	27,800	19,443	47,243
25	55	19,850	28,061	47,911
30	60	12,600	39,065	51,665
35	65	None	53,110	53,110

BUT THE ESTATE VALUE IS LESS THAN THE $50,000 LEVEL COVERAGE OF THE WHOLE-LIFE PLAN!

You can correct this by purchasing more than $50,000 to start with. For example, $60,000 would be $205 per year, or only $32.50 more than for $50,000. This would maintain $50,000 or more at all times, and even though you would have $32.50 less per year for your bonds, you would still have $50,028 in bonds at age 65 and again beat the whole-life policy. Term insurance by itself is so inexpensive that there is no reason for your family to be underprotected. Another choice would be to invest your money where it could be expected to earn more than 5%.

BUT ARE THESE OTHER INVESTMENTS GUARANTEED?

Reliance on guarantees has cost people more money than you can possibly imagine. As mentioned earlier, guaranteed plans can assure you of a given number of dollars, but you do not have any assurance that you will be able to pay the higher prices. Dollars alone aren't the answer; they don't wear very well and they taste horrible. They must be exchanged for food and clothing, and if your stockpile of dollars is insufficient to pay for the things you need, you will be in deep trouble and have to get along on less. Even the life insurance industry is finally admitting that guaranteed dollars aren't the answer.

WHERE CAN I EXPECT TO EARN MORE THAN 5% WITHOUT EXCESSIVE RISK?

You can buy stocks of growing, well-managed companies. Specific results aren't guaranteed, but studies show an average growth rate of about 9% per year. If you don't care to select and manage your own stocks, you can invest in mutual funds and let professional money managers select and supervise your investments. Well selected real estate has been profitable for many people.

The main thing to keep in mind is that it is very possible to earn more than 5% or 6% on your money—and without speculating. Your library has books on investments. The investment dealers in your community will be able to help you find ways to put your money to work in sound, conservative investments. Just realize that the over-glorified cash value life insurance is about the world's worst way of accumulating money for future use.

Many people fail to realize how an increase of 1% or 2% per year can improve their financial situation. They compare 3% with 5%, for example, conclude that the difference is only 2% and do nothing about it because 2% isn't worth the trouble. What they don't realize is that money working at 5% is producing 66.7% more interest than money earning only 3%. If this sounds unbelievable, divide the difference of 2% by the 3% rate. The percentage is 66.7%.

Series E bonds are now earning 6% if held to maturity. If this rate continues, your results of a term and invest plan would outpace cash value life insurance even more than previously illustrated. At a conservative 5% growth rate for Series E bonds, the annual difference of $560 for 35 years would grow to $53,110. At 6%, the final value would be $66,147, or $13,037 more. This seemingly insignificant difference of 1% per year would give you almost 25% more ending value from age 30 to 65. Compound interest is wonderful, especially when it is working for *you* and not the life insurance company.

A handy thing to know is the Rule of 72. This is a simple way to find out how long it takes a lump sum of money to double in value at a given rate of interest. Just divide 72 by the interest rate; the answer is the number of years needed to double your money. For example:

Interest Rate	Years to Double
3%	24
4%	18
5%	14.4
6%	12
7%	10.3
8%	9
9%	8
10%	7.2

Another application of the Rule of 72 will determine

the growth rate of an investment. Just divide 72 by the number of years that it took for money to double in value. For example, if your money doubled in ten years, it would have been working at 7.2% per year. This is a handy rule, isn't it?

NOTE: Mutual funds frequently show past records of a lump-sum investment for periods of ten years. The amount illustrated is usually $10,000. Check the ten-year records of different mutual funds and you will find that many of them have doubled or better in the average ten-year period. Past records are no guarantee of future results, but mutual funds are worth considering as a place to invest that money you don't pay for cash-value life insurance.

INSTEAD OF BUYING DECREASING TERM TO AGE 65, WHY CAN'T I BUY LEVEL TERM?

You can, and you have at least two choices. At age 30, you can buy $50,000 of level term to age 65 for an annual premium of $422.00, or $310.50 less than the whole-life premium of $732.50. Both your premium and your insurance coverage would remain constant for 35 years. If you put the difference into Series E bonds earning at least 5%, the value of your estate would increase with each bond that you bought. Here is what would happen:

End of Year	Your Age	Value of Bonds @ 5%	Level Term Coverage	Total Estate Value
5	35	$ 1,800	$50,000	$51,800
10	40	4,101	50,000	54,101
15	45	7,035	50,000	57,035
20	50	10,780	50,000	60,780
25	55	15,559	50,000	65,559
30	60	21,660	50,000	71,660
35	65	29,448	——	29,448

The combination of level term to age 65 and a separate investment would not give you as much cash as the combination of decreasing term and a separate investment. However, it would still be more than the whole-life cash value of $27,750.

Another advantage of this approach would be an increasing estate value. The whole life plan which would provide a constant $50,000, including an ever-increasing "deductible"—your cash value. The level term plan would provide $50,000 of true insurance coverage plus your investment. For example, if you were to die at age 60, your family would receive $71,660 with this method, as opposed to $50,000 from the whole-life policy.

NOTE: Since the level term to age 65 premium remains the same for 35 years, you would be overpaying in the early years to build up a reserve within the policy to offset the higher mortality costs in the later years. There is nothing wrong about a level term to age 65 policy; just be sure you understand the difference between "level-premium level-term" and "increasing-premium level-term" (renewable term).

WHY NOT BUY RENEWABLE TERM AND THEN RENEW ONLY WHAT I NEED?

Now you're thinking! This would be your choice if you liked the idea of being able to control the face amount of your insurance. Decreasing term will diminish at a scheduled rate each year, which may be faster than your net worth is increasing. Also, you might incur larger obligations, such as a bigger home mortgage, that you would want to have covered by life insurance. Another consideration is inflation. It's reasonably certain that prices will be higher ten years from now than at present. You may also incur financial reverses that would temporarily reduce your savings or investments. In other words, renewable level term would provide the flexibility that you might need.

You would have a choice of yearly renewable term, five-year renewable or ten-year renewable. The plan you select should be renewable to at least age 70 without evidence of insurability and convertible to age 65, also without evidence of insurability. To keep the arithmetic reasonably simple, let's say that you select ten-year renewable and convertible level term; that you evaluate your position each ten years, and renew only the amount needed to maintain an estate value of at least $50,000. Each year you would invest the difference between the term premium and the whole-life premium of $732.50 in Series E bonds earning 5% per year. Here is how this would work out:

	Years 1-10	Years 11-20	Years 21-30	Years 31-35
Amount of insurance	$50,000	$42,160	$30,447	$13,374
Annual premium	139.00	219.11	371.10	394.40
Annual investment	593.50	513.39	361.40	338.10
Value of bonds at end of period				
Bonds bought during latest 10-year period	7,840	6,782	4,774	1,961 (5 yrs)
Bonds bought during earlier 10-year periods	———	12,771	31,852	46,734
Total value of bonds	7,840	19,553	36,626	48,694
Amount of insurance to be renewed	42,160	30,447	13,374	1,306*

By this method you would always have an estate value of at least $50,000. If you were to die just prior to an evaluation date, your estate value would be more than $50,000. For example, if you died just before the tenth year, the insurance protection would be $50,000; the bond value would be $7,840 for a total of $57,840 for your family.

You will also note that your insurance premium never exceeds the $732.50 that you would be charged for the whole-life plan. The last renewal at age 60 would be only $394.40—$338.10 less than for whole life bought at age 30. Another point to keep in mind is that this illustration is based on a growth rate of only 5%. If your money earned more than 5%, you would need less insurance than the amounts illustrated.

At age 65, you would have almost as much cash as with the decreasing term method ($48,694 vs. $53,110). You

---

*It is doubtful you would want to renew only $1,306 of insurance since it is such a small amount. You could continue to have $13,374 of protection to age 70.

could continue to have $13,374 of insurance to age 70 for only $394.40 per year if you wanted it. You could convert the term policy at age 65 to $13,374 of whole life for a guaranteed annual premium of $948.00.

BUT IF I BOUGHT THE WHOLE LIFE AT AGE 30, I WOULD HAVE $50,000 AT AGE 65 FOR ONLY $732.50 PER YEAR!

Correction! You would have $50,000 *including your cash value of $27,750*, for a net protection of $22,250. If you continued to pay the whole-life premium of $732.50, you would have no income from the cash value. If you wanted the use of the $27,750 of cash value, it would cost you $1,387.50 per year for interest, plus the premium of $732.50, for a total annual cost of $2,120 for $22,250 of insurance. This figures out to $95.28 per $1000 of protection. And the premium for whole life bought at age 65 is only $70.10 per $1,000! If you were to convert the term policy to $13,374 of whole life at age 65, you would have an estate value of $62,068. ($13,374 of whole life plus $48,694 in bonds equals $62,068). This is $12,068 more than the whole-life policy bought at age 30.

Actually, you should have no need to convert to whole life since your bonds would be worth almost as much as the face amount of the whole-life policy. ($48,694 in bonds vs. $50,000 face amount). However, if you wanted to leave $13,374 to your favorite charity, you would be guaranteed a way of doing it.

BUT IF I BOUGHT THE WHOLE LIFE AT AGE 30, I COULD CONVERT TO PAID-UP INSURANCE AT AGE 65!

Okay, let's look at this idea which is a favorite pitch of the cash-value advocates. The $50,000 whole-life policy bought at age 30 would have a paid-up value of $39,350 at age 65. You could stop paying premiums and have $39,350 of insurance for the rest of your life. However, this would include the $27,750 of cash value. The difference between the paid-up value and the cash value is $11,600 of actual protection. Since the $27,750 would be tied up in the policy, you would be losing the earning power of this money. At 5%, this would amount to $1,387.50 per year. This would be your cost for $11,600 of insurance. When you divide $1,387.50 by 11.6, you find that the cost per $1,000 of protection is $119.61.

In comparison, you could buy $11,600 of whole life at age 65 for an annual premium of only $823. At 5%, the interest from your $48,694 in bonds would amount to $2,434.70 per year, which would more than pay the premium for $11,600 of whole life bought at age 65.

Don't overlook the fact that this plan of renewable term and bonds would produce $48,694 in cashable bonds at age 65, which is $9,344 more than the paid up value at age 65 of the whole-life plan bought at age 30.

HOW ABOUT USING THE EXTENDED-TERM OPTION AT AGE 65?

If you did this, you would have $50,000 of insurance for about fourteen years and would have no more premiums to pay. If you lived beyond fourteen years, your family would receive nothing from the insurance company. Also, you would receive no income from the $27,750 cash value if you converted the whole-life policy to extended term.

In comparison, the renewable term bond plan would leave an inheritance of $48,694 if you spent the annual income of $2,434.70 (assuming 5% interest) and did not touch the principal. If you did not spend the interest income, but just let the interest accumulate at 5%, your bonds would be worth $98,394 at the end of fourteen years.

BUT IF I DON'T SAVE THE DIFFERENCE, I END UP AT AGE 65 WITH NOTHING.

A flippant answer could be: "Then buy term and *enjoy* the difference." At least you would have the satisfaction of knowing that you were not overpaying for your family's protection.

More seriously, whether you do or don't save the difference is completely your own decision and responsibility. If you are so irresponsible and weak that you cannot save a part of each paycheck on your own, then go ahead—buy cash-value life insurance and let the insurance company get the benefit of your hard-earned dollars. You will have no trouble finding a salesman who will be overjoyed to sell you this glorious, guaranteed way to riches. Just accept his sales pitch as gospel and help him fatten his bank account and his company's coffers. Just ignore everything you have read so far and the fact that a little gumption on your part can provide more money for your family if you die and more money for you if you live.

WHY CAN'T I BUY PERMANENT INSURANCE AND THEN BORROW THE CASH VALUE TO INVEST?

You can—if you want to pay interest for the use of your own money, if you want to overpay for protection, if you believe that a 2½% or 3½% savings account will be enough for future financial needs. Thousands of people are doing this without realizing the true costs involved. They have been led to believe that borrowing their cash value at 5% when the banks and other credit institutions are charging 6%, 7% and 8% is very sound business. Also, they have been told that borrowing their cash value at 5% and reinvesting at a higher rate makes good sense. However, when you dig into this idea, it proves to be very costly.

To illustrate, let's say that you bought the $50,000 of whole life at age 30 for a premium of $732.50. You are now age 40 and the policy has a cash/loan value of $5,550. You decide to borrow this money.

The first result is that the death benefit of your $50,000 whole-life policy drops to $44,450 the instant that you borrow the cash value. The second result is that you now have an annual interest cost of $277.50 (5% of $5,550). This is in addition to your premium of $732.50—a total annual cost of $1,010. When you divide $1,010 by 44.450, you find that your cost of protection is $22.72 per $1,000.

NOTE: You don't have to actually borrow the cash value and actually pay the 5% interest to be paying $22.72 per $1,000 of protection. Even if you leave the money with the insurance company, you are still losing the interest (at least 5% per year) that the money would earn elsewhere. And let me point out again that although the insurance company pays or rather adds a minimal interest to your cash value, you are not benefiting. The insurance company benefits since each increase in cash value decreases the protection and consequently the company's risk.

The question to be answered is: "Is there a better way to use your $5,550 of cash and a yearly outlay of $1,010?" Try this for size:

At age 40, you can buy decreasing term to age 65 for $4.86 per $1,000 or ten-year renewable and convertible level term for $5.01 per $1,000. The interest cost alone ($277.50) would buy these amounts of honest protection:

$55,000 of decreasing term to age 65

$53,393 of 10-year renewable and convertible level term

In other words, if you put the $5,550 cash value to work at 5%, the interest alone would provide more death protection than the whole-life policy bought ten years ago. In addition, you would have your present premium of $732.50 to use in other ways.

A second idea would be to buy $44,450 of term insurance. At age 40, the annual premiums would be:

$226.02 for $44,450 of decreasing term to age 65

$232.69 for $44,450 of 10-year renewable and convertible level term

You will note that the annual premium for either type of term insurance is less than the interest of $277.50 you would be paying for the use of your own money.

The theme of this book is not "Buy term and invest the difference." However, many buyers have been brainwashed into believing that permanent life insurance is the greatest of all investment plans. The mutual life insurance companies have been particularly strong proponents of the investment qualities of cash value insurance. By emphasizing the *"guesstimated"* dividends of their participating policies, they have conned many buyers into overpaying for their life insurance.

You have been advised to buy only non-participating insurance, and the figures used to illustrate the advantages of term insurance plus a separate investment are all non-par figures. To help you better understand why you should avoid dividend-promising policies, let's examine a typical proposal for $50,000 of whole life for a man age 30 offered by a major mutual life insurance company.

Face amount	$50,000
Issue age	Male, age 30
Annual premium	$976.00

You will recall that the annual premium for $50,000 of non-par whole life is $732.50, or $243.50 less than for this par policy. This is about a 33% overcharge by the mutual company.

Cash value at age 65	$ 27,950.00
Accumulated dividends at age 65	34,450.00
Total cash available at age 65	$ 62,400.00
Total premiums paid to age 65	−34,160.00
Total profit at age 65	$ 28,240.00
Average profit per year	$ 806.86 (28,240 divided by 35 yrs)
Average percent return per year	82.7% ($806.86 divided by $976)

Isn't this a fantastic bargain? Where else can you buy such a wonderful plan? Do you know of any other way to earn 82.7% on your money each and every year for 35 years? Wouldn't you really rather have a $100,000 plan?

Let's take another look at this proposal.

First, note that the guaranteed cash value of $27,950 is only $200 more than the $27,750 of the non-par whole life. The mutual companies like to have you believe that their policies develop much higher cash values than the non-par policies of the stock companies. 'T ain't so. With this insignificant difference in cash value at age 65, it is obvious that the annual overcharge of $243.50 is almost completely designed to furnish the money for those wonderful dividends.

Next, note that the guaranteed cash value of $27,950 has been combined with nonguaranteed dividends of $34,450. This sales technique implies that both amounts are equally certain to be there at your age 65 for a grand total of $62,400 and a profit of $28,240.

The cash value is a definite and guaranteed amount, and there is no question that you would have at least $27,950 cash surrender value at age 65. However, in order for you to have $34,450 of accumulated dividends at age 65, you would have to receive an annual refund of $251.03 each and every year from age 31 to age 65. Furthermore, this refund would have to earn 7% per year, compounded annually to equal $34,450. This is a bit far-fetched!

The average life insurance buyer just accepts these figures as gospel, buys this wonderful money-maker, and goes blithely on his way, entranced by the thought of all the money he is going to have at retirement time. To help you be an above-average life insurance buyer, here is the arithmetic needed to check the salesman's dazzling figurework:

NOTE: You can avoid this exercise by resolving to buy only non-par term insurance from a stock company, but if you are curious, you will need a compound-interest table (included in the appendix) pencil, and paper. Here is how to proceed:

Turn to the table headed "Accumulation of One Dollar Deposited at the Beginning of Each Year." Next note the factors for 34 years in the columns headed 4%, 5%, 6%, and 8%. The reason for using 34 years rather than 35 is that there is at least a one-year delay before the first dividend is paid. These factors are:

4%	72.6522
5%	89.3203
6%	110.4348
7%	137.2370 (not listed in this table)
8%	171.3168

The next step is to divide the estimated dividends of $34,450 by each of these factors. The answer is the amount of money that would have to be invested each year at these various interest rates to be worth $34,450 at the end of thirty-four years. In other words, this is the annual dividend that would need to be paid each and every year. Here are the amounts:

Assumed Rate of Interest	Annual Dividend Required
4%	$474.18
5%	385.69
6%	311.95
7%	251.03
8%	201.09

Which combination of assumed interest rate and annual dividend would you like to believe? If you believe any of them, perhaps you had better start selling life insurance so you can get others started on this wonderful road to riches.

If you disbelieve these figures (and hopefully, you do), here is why.

We have established that the initial overcharge for dividends is at least $243.50 when compared with a non-par whole life. If you had bought the non-par plan, you would have received an immediate and guaranteed "dividend" of $243.50 per year from age 30 to age 65. You could have used this money in any way you chose but for simplicity's sake, let's assume you just kept it in your checking account where it earned no interest.

Now let's compare your checking account buildup with the dividends promised by this mutual life insurance company. These amounts are the cash dividends "guesstimated" and are not the accumulated dividends.

NOTE: "Cumulative" and "accumulated" are not synonymous. Cumulative is a running total without interest; accumulated is a running total including interest.

Policy Year	Cumulative Overcharge @ 243.50 per yr.	Cumulative Illustrated Dividends	Difference
1	$ 243.50	$ None	$243.50
2	487.00	106.00	381.00
3	730.50	242.50	488.00
4	974.00	409.50	564.50
5	1,217.50	607.50	610.00
6	1,461.00	837.00	624.00
7	1,704.50	1,099.00	605.50
8	1,948.00	1,394.00	554.00
9	2,191.50	1,724.50	467.00
10	2,435.00	2,090.50	344.50
11	2,678.50	2,475.00	203.50
12	2,922.00	2,878.50	43.50
13	3,165.00	3,300.00	(135.00)

Hurray! After thirteen years, the illustrated dividends finally exceed the cumulative overcharge by $135.00. Aren't you deliriously happy that you listened to the salesman? Where else but a mutual life insurance company could you pay so much for so little? Doesn't it make you feel benevolent to have given over $3,000 to the insurance company with no charge to them? They need your money so badly!

The previous comparison of non-par whole life and decreasing term to age 65 plus a separate bond-buying program showed the tremendous advantage of buying only protection from an insurance company. Here is a similar comparison based on this participating whole life plan:

	Participating Whole Life	Term Plus 5% Bonds
Annual premium (Age 30)	$ 976.00	$ 172.50
Annual difference	none	803.50
Total per year	$ 976.00	$ 976.00
Total paid to age 65 (35 X $976)	34,160.00	34,160.00
Guaranted cash value at age 65	27,950.00	none
Accumulated dividends at age 65*	34,450.00	none
Value of bonds at age 65	none	76,203.94
Profit at age 65	$28,240.00	$42,043.94
Difference in results		$13,803.94 more

*Remember that these are "guesstimates," not guarantees.

103

Even if the asinine illustrated dividends were to materialize, you would be better off with the term insurance program. Right?

Series E bonds were used in this discussion to illustrate that even a relatively low-yielding investment of only 5% would provide better results than cash-value life insurance. Since this is not a book on investing, no attempt is being made to recommend any specific form of investment. The key point for you to remember is to avoid cash-value life insurance as a method of accumulating money for future needs.

To avoid complicated calculations, this discussion of "Term and Invest" has been presented with no adjustment for the probable higher prices of the future. The dirty word is INFLATION, which has been with us for so long that we accept it without really understanding it.

Simply stated, inflation is the fact that each dollar buys less as time goes on. With each dollar buying less and less, we need to have more dollars to maintain the same buying power.

Cash-value life insurance can guarantee you a given number of dollars at a given point in time. However, you have absolutely no guarantee that this stated number of dollars will be enough to offset inflation. If you base your plans on bread costing 50 cents a loaf when you retire and then have to pay a dollar a loaf, your only solution is to get by on half a loaf. In other words, the only thing guaranteed by cash-value life insurance is continual erosion of its investment component.

We don't know what rate of inflation the future will bring. Until recently it averaged about 3% per year, but now it has exceeded that rate quite substantially. To give you an idea of the effect of varying rates of inflation, study these figures:

Number of Years	Rate of Inflation		
	4 Percent	6 Percent	8 Percent
Present value	$1.00	$1.00	$1.00
10 years	.68	.56	.46
15 years	.56	.42	.32
20 years	.46	.31	.21
25 years	.38	.23	.15
30 years	.31	.17	.10

These are not just meaningless numbers that can be disregarded. To illustrate, let's say that inflation averages 4% per year over the next twenty years. On this basis, a dollar would be worth 46 cents and you would need twice as many dollars as at present just to stay even. If the inflation rate were to average 6% per year, your dollar would be worth 31 cents. You would therefore need more than three times as much.

NOTE: The "official" inflation rate for 1973 was close to 9%.

Inflation also has to be considered in the selection of term insurance. If you buy only decreasing term, you are running a risk that this will decline faster than your family's needs. Level term provides a constant death benefit and can be adjusted to fit your requirements. If you build up enough assets to keep up with inflation, you can reduce the size of your policy accordingly. Your family may need only $500 per month (plus Social Security) at present, but you don't know how much prices will rise in the future. They could very well need an additional $200 per month ten years from now. Level term gives you the flexibility needed for your family's financial needs.

From 1968 to 1975, inflation totaled about 51%. As a result, 1968 life insurance dollars will not provide the same quantity of food, shelter or clothing in 1975 as in 1968. The figures below illustrate this drastic reduction:

Life Insurance Face Value in 1968	Estimated Buying Power in 1975	Additional Insurance Needed in 1975 to Restore 1968 Buying Power
$ 10,000	$ 6,500	$ 5,450
20,000	12,950	10,850
30,000	19,450	16,300
40,000	25,950	21,700
50,000	32,400	27,150
100,000	64,800	54,250

In terms of monthly income, here is more food for thought:

Monthly Income 1968	Estimated Buying Power in 1975
$ 600	$390
700	455
800	520
900	585
1000	650
1200	780
1500	970

CHAPTER TEN

WHAT TO DO

Are you becoming somewhat skeptical of the so-called benefits of cash-value life insurance? If so, you are on the right track.

If you are just starting your life insurance program, you are also in luck, because you now know what to look for and how to avoid overpaying for your family's protection.

If you have previously been sold the wrong type of life insurance, don't kick yourself for not getting smarter sooner. You can very likely take advantage of your new-found knowledge.

Do not hesitate to admit that you made a bad buy. Too many husbands and fathers have been steered away from honest, low-cost protection and been sold cash values and dividends instead. In countless cases, the widows and orphans are suffering the consequences. Don't let it happen to your wife and children!

You have probably been told that your permanent insurance is the most precious possession you have, that it's practically sacred—along with God, the flag and motherhood—besides being the best investment you ever made. You can believe this sales pitch if you want to, or if you are too proud or too stubborn to change your thinking. How long will your pride and stubbornness support your family after your death?

If you are honest with yourself, you should realize that it is downright ridiculous to consider a life insurance policy so untouchable that you must never, never think of replacing it. If you bought a car that was a lemon, you would unload it the first chance you had. We replace just about everything else we have—cars, homes, boats, furniture, even spouses. What is so unique about a life insurance policy that you should hold onto it when is isn't doing the job you want it to—provide adequate protection at a reasonable cost?

Your most important consideration is your insurability. DO NOT let your present insurance lapse until you get new insurance, have the new policy in your possession and have paid the first premium. Only then should you drop your present insurance.

If you have doubts about your insurability because of your health, do not make a formal application for new insurance. Instead, ask the salesman to submit a "trial application" or "inquiry." This is not the same as applying for life insurance. Once you have submitted a formal application to a company and have been declined or offered a "rated" policy, you are a marked man from then on. On any subsequent application, you must state what happened. If you don't report this information, you will be guilty of misrepresentation.

An "inquiry" is not an application. Even if the reply to your request for information states that you cannot qualify for insurance at a standard premium, you have not been legally declined nor offered a "rated" or "substandard" policy.

Renewable term and decreasing term premiums may be increased by "tables" because of health or other reasons. Each table is a 25% increase over the normal or standard premium and may be identified with letters (A, B, C, D, etc.) or by numbers (1, 2, 3, 4, etc.) Table A and Table 1 both mean a 25% increase over the standard premium. For example, if the standard premium is $4.00 per $1,000, a Table A or 1 would be an additional charge of $1.00 per $1,000. (25% of $4.00); Table B or 2 would be a $2.00 increase, etc.

Just because one company refuses to sell you insurance at a standard premium, is no reason for you to be discouraged or to start calling an undertaker. There have been cases where one company declined to sell a person insurance at any price and another company accepted the same person at standard rates. An independent agent will be able to contact more than one company in case of an adverse reply.

Companies have been known to offer permanent insurance at a standard premium but refuse to sell you term insurance without a rating. This is simply a device to try to force you to overpay. If this happens to you, just tell them "Thanks, but no thanks."

A rated policy may still be a good buy in comparison with what you are now paying. The rating may be only temporary, such as for two years, and then drop to standard. Even if the policy does not provide for an automatic reduction at some future date, there is still a possibility that the rating can be reduced or removed in later years. Most companies will review a rated policy after one year.

Once you have accepted a rated policy, the company cannot raise the table rating in later years, even if your health worsens. If the policy is issued with a Table 2, for example, (50% over standard), the premiums for future years will also remain at Table 2.

NOTE: Decreasing term is normally issued with a constant or level premium that remains the same for the life of the policy. Renewable term premiums increase in later years, but the beginning table rating is not increased.

You may also be rated for hazardous activities such as flying, skin diving, auto racing, etc. This form of rating is usually identified as a "flat extra" of so much per $1,000, such as $5.00. If you cease this risky activity and so notify the company, you can usually have this form of rating removed since it is not based on your physical condition.

To repeat, don't be discouraged by one company's refusal to insure you at a standard premium. Don't forget the "trial application" route if you have doubts about your insurability.

IF I CAN'T GET NEW INSURANCE AT A REASONABLE PREMIUM, SHOULD I CONVERT MY PRESENT INSURANCE TO EXTENDED TERM AND THEN INVEST THE PREMIUM?

This is a possible solution that would depend upon the length of the extended term period and what your premium could earn during the extended term period.

Let's say you now have a $10,000 whole-life policy with an annual premium of $200 and an extended term value of twenty years. If you convert the policy to extended term, your family would have $10,000 of protection for twenty years and you would have $200 per year to invest. Here is what $200 per year will grow to at various rates of interest:

Interest Rate	20th Year Value
5%	$ 6,944
6%	7,799
7%	8,773
8%	9,885
10%	12,600

If you died before the twenty years was up, your family would receive the $10,000 plus the value of the investment. If you lived beyond twenty years, they would receive only the investment.

There is no absolute answer to this question. You would have to evaluate your own particular situation and make your own decision. If you were to follow such a course, you would have to save $200 each and every year. In general, the longer the extended term period, the lower the risk because the time element is an all-important requirement for accumulating money.

HOW ABOUT CONVERTING TO PAID-UP INSURANCE AND THEN INVESTING MY PREMIUM?

This method is advisable only if the reduced amount would be enough to cover your obligations to your family. If you have a $10,000 policy with a paid-up value of $4,000, a change to paid-up insurance would immediately reduce your family's protection by $6,000. It isn't advisable to risk your family's welfare in this manner. A better choice would be to keep your present insurance in force, borrow the cash value and invest it where is could earn more than your interest costs. If the loan rate on your policy is 5% and you can invest this money at 6%, you will come out ahead over a period of time. Here is an illustration based on $1,000:

End of Year	Value of $1,000 @ 6%	Cumulative Interest @ 5%	Net Gain
1	$1,060	$ 50	$ 10
5	1,338	250	85
10	1,791	500	291
15	2,397	750	647
20	3,207	1,000	1,207

The interest cost of $50 per year would be deductible on you income tax return and would reduce your effective cost to less than 5%. If your money was invested in tax-exempt securities, the income would not be taxable to you. Series E bonds at 6% would involve no current taxes. If invested in growth-type stocks or mutual funds, you would incur only a small amount of taxable income since these types of investments usually have a low dividend rate. Their main attraction is the possible appreciation over a period of years.

NOTE: Just a seemingly insignificant difference of 1% per year can be profitable for you over a period of time. Remember that an increase from 5% to 6% is actually an increase of 20% in the earning power of your money.

HOW DO I GO ABOUT SELECTING A PARTICULAR INSURANCE COMPANY FOR MY TERM INSURANCE?

First, forget about the mutual companies and their "guesstimated" dividends. There is no reason for you to give them extra money for nothing so that they can pay it back to you at whatever rate they decide best fits their scheme of things. In short, consider stock companies only.

The Appendix lists typical premiums for various forms of term insurance and includes the names and home office addresses of the companies whose rates are quoted. These are some of the best rates I know of, but are not guaranteed to be the absolute best. If you aren't able to locate a local agency in the Yellow Pages, call or write to the home office for their nearest agency. According to the Pennsylvania Insurance Department, the cost of term life insurance varies by as much as 140%. Obviously, it pays to shop.

Verify that the company you are considering is registered in your state; you can do this through your state insurance department. You may be able to obtain other information about the company at the same time, but the main point is to be sure that your state has approved the company to operate there.

When you decide to check on a company, be certain to get its full and exact name. With over 1,800 life insurance companies in business today, there are several with similar-sounding names. There are at least fifteen companies with the word "American" in their names; at least five that have "Banker" as a part of their name; about nine that include the name of "Lincoln."

The Alfred M. Best Company (P.O. Box 600, Morristown, N.J. 07960) reviews most American and Canadian life insurance companies for soundness, stability, permanence of operation, and safety from the viewpoint of the policyholder. If Best's analysis is favorable, the company is placed on their "Recommended List." The number of recommended companies varies from year to year, but it seems that about 25% of the companies surveyed meet Best's criteria. This is not an absolute guarantee of a company's soundness, but is fairly reliable. If a company is on this list, their agents usually have a summary of the Best analysis. Ask them for a copy.

SHOULD I GO BACK TO THE SAME AGENT WHO SOLD ME MY PRESENT INSURANCE?

Would you go back to a car dealer or an appliance dealer who sold you a lemon? You can go back to the same agent if you want to, but don't expect the maximum cooperation or assistance. He isn't very likely to admit that he sold you the wrong type of insurance in the beginning, and will do his best to defend what he sold.

He will probably try to convince you to convert your present insurance to extended term or paid-up insurance so that his sales record won't be blemished by a lapsed policy. He may try to persuade you to use your accumulated dividends to buy some more of that wonderful cash-value insurance so that he can get another juicy commission. With his own self-interest in mind, he may try to have you borrow your present cash value to pay the premium for new insurance with his company.

If he is a salesman of a mutual company, he may offer you participating term and show you the bait of all the guesstimated dividends you might receive. Participating term is about as ridiculous as you can get. Your reason for buying term insurance is to get the maximum protection per dollar of premium. When the premium includes an overcharge for future dividends, you again overpay for protection.

If you feel you can convince him that you want only pure protection term insurance without any "goodies," go ahead and call him. But be prepared for some static.

IS THERE ANY ADVANTAGE IN REPLACING OLD PERMANENT INSURANCE WITH NEW PERMANENT INSURANCE?

Yes, for the salesman. He will receive another first-year commission.

However, it is completely possible that you can buy new whole life for a lower cost per $1,000 of protection than you are now paying for a permanent policy that is several years old. If the old policy was based on an outdated mortality table, a new policy using more up-to-date mortality costs would cost you less. Also, if the old policy was a par policy and the new one is non-par, you could get new permanent insurance for a lower cost than your old policy.

This is a shady trick of some salesmen. Non-par rates have been reduced quite substantially in recent years while the par rates of the mutual companies are still high. With a little fancy figurework, a salesman can show you how to have new permanent insurance for less money than you are now paying. Don't fall for this pitch; it's no bargain for you. Change to term insurance; that's your best buy.

IF I DON'T GO BACK TO MY ORIGINAL AGENT, HOW SHOULD I GO ABOUT SELECTING AN AGENT?

Go to an independent life insurance broker who is licensed with several different companies and is able to sell you the type of insurance that you want.

The Yellow Pages of your telephone directory lists many different life insurance agencies. Many of these represent only one company and are not permitted to sell other companies' products. Because of this limitation, they know very little about competitors' plans. Avoid these "captive salesmen."

After weeding out the single-company agencies, start calling some of the others that appear to be independents. Ask for the head of the agency and verify that he *is* independent. Tell him that you want to buy some term insurance and ask him if you can buy it from him. If you have a specific company in mind, ask if he is licensed with that company. If you are fairly certain of the type and amount that you want, ask him for prices. He may be willing to give you this information over the phone, but it would be advisable to ask him for a written description of the plan. He may also be able to supply a specimen policy for you to study and review.

NOTE: Some companies have slightly lower rates for term insurance when it is attached as a "rider" to some form of permanent insurance. In order to buy at these reduced rates, you must first buy a given amount of cash value insurance. The mutual companies push this combination and pay the salesman a higher commission than for an all term policy. In case you are offered such a plan don't take it.

General insurance agencies that sell mainly auto and homeowner insurance sometimes have a life department. In many cases, their life insurance business is secondary to their casualty insurance business. Because it is actually a part-time affair, agencies such as these are frequently no more knowledgeable about life insurance than the single-company agencies.

There are independent agencies that are also licensed

to sell stocks, bonds, mutual funds and other securities. As a general rule, these dual-licensed salesmen are more term-insurance oriented than those who sell insurance only. They realize the value of separating your protection from your investment, and they don't try to persuade you to buy cash values and dividends.

There are sales organizations that offer both investment and life insurance. Although they are usually strong supporters of term insurance, their rates are not always the best buys. Also, these salesmen are sometimes limited to selling the life insurance of only one company, and therefore are not true independents.

The trust department of your bank may also be able to steer you to an independent salesman who is not reluctant to sell term insurance.

This will all take time and you will probably have to wade through a sea of insurance double talk to get the coverage you need. "Term" is still a four-letter word with many salesmen, so don't expect to find a superabundance of term insurance advocates. You will probably have to do some digging on your own, but it will be worth it. Good luck!

IF I DECIDE TO BUY NEW TERM INSURANCE, IS THERE ANYTHING ELSE THAT I SHOULD BE AWARE OF?

Whenever you buy new life insurance, you automatically start a new suicide period of two years. If you commit suicide during this two-year period, the company will not pay off. Your family will receive only the premiums you have paid. After the two years, death by suicide would be covered.

When you buy new insurance, you also start a new "contestable" period of two years. If you were to conceal information about your health or personal activities when you applied for the insurance and then were to die within two years because of this concealed information, the company could legally refuse to pay the death claim. This does *not* mean that your death within two years would not be covered. The company must prove that you *knowingly* withheld information and that your application would have been disapproved if they had known the true situation. As long as you are completely honest, the contestable clause is nothing for you to worry about.

NOTE: There have been cases where a person applying for insurance has told the salesman the full story of his medical history and hazardous activities such as flying, scuba diving, auto racing, etc., but the salesman has neglected to include it in the application. *When you sign the application, be sure that it is accurate and complete.* This also applies to the medical examination. Every life insurance policy includes a copy of the original application and the medical questionnaire. Be sure to check these items to be certain that they are complete and factual.

SHOULD I NOTIFY MY PRESENT INSURANCE COMPANY THAT I AM REPLACING THEIR POLICY?

You will have to in order to get your money back, but you don't need to notify them immediately.

The application form for new insurance will probably include a question asking if the insurance being applied for will replace or modify present insurance and the names of the companies involved. If this is your intent, you should answer yes.

When your application reaches the home office of the new company, they will notify your present company of your intention. This may trigger a letter from your present company telling you what a horrible mistake you are making in getting rid of that precious permanent insurance and advising you to reconsider. You may also be visited by the company's agent and you can, but need not, discuss your decision with him. It's your choice. If you do elect to meet him, he will quite likely do his best to change your mind about term insurance. If unsuccessful, he may offer to sell you term insurance with *his* company. A good response to an offer like this is to ask him why you weren't offered term insurance in the beginning.

IS THERE ANY LEGAL REASON WHY I SHOULD NOT REPLACE MY PRESENT INSURANCE?

Absolutely none!

More and more people are realizing that cash-value life insurance is a bad buy and are replacing these outmoded, high-cost policies with modern, low-cost term insurance. Because of this trend, the cash-value lobbyists have forced through "Replacement Regulations" in several states. The alleged purpose of these regulations is to protect the consumer. The real purpose is to preserve cash-value insurance now in force.

If your state has a replacement regulation, this does not mean that you can be forced to keep a policy that you don't want. The target of these regulations is the salesman selling term insurance as a replacement for permanent insurance. His license is controlled by the state, and if he doesn't comply with the provisions of the replacement regulation, he can be delicensed and put out of business.

The replacement regulations require a replacing salesman to complete an involved and unintelligible "Comparison Statement" when he proposes new term insurance that will change existing insurance. By this method, the cash-value advocates hope to create such a mountain of paperwork for the term salesman that he will not recommend replacement even when it is the logical thing to do.

Not only is the paperwork involved and meaningless "insurancese," but the required forms are also constructed and phrased to emphasize the supposed benefits of cash-value insurance. If you have been confused about life insurance in the past, wait until you have been exposed to the jumble of information required by the replacement regulations!

You certainly should receive a full and complete explanation of both present and proposed insurance. If the salesman you contact won't do this—and in writing—find another one who will. However, it is completely unfair to require a salesman to support and explain his product using rules and regulations established by the opposition. This is comparable to demanding that a Ford salesman demonstrate and prove his car to you according to rules laid down by General Motors!

The really ridiculous feature of the replacement regulations is that there is no equivalent protection for you when you start your life insurance program or buy additional insurance. All this concern for you—the poor, unprotected buyer—comes into play only when there is a possibility that you might drop or change that super-sacred cash-value insurance policy.

Instead of replacement regulations, the real need is for a "Suitability" or "Full Disclosure" law that would require all insurance salesmen to provide full and complete information about both term and cash-value insurance whenever you buy life insurance. We have a "Truth-in-Lending" law. Why shouldn't we have a "Truth-in-Insurance" law? Can you just imagine the wails of the cash-value advocates if such a law were to be put on the books? The sound would be deafening!

NOTE: Some cash-value salesmen refer to term insurance salesmen as "termites." Another title is "twister," which may be used by the cash-value salesman whose policy has been replaced by a "termite." His implication is that all termites are twisters. 'T ain't so! A life insurance salesman is said to be "twisting" if he uses misrepresentation or an incomplete comparison to induce a replacement to the detriment of the policyholder. If he provides an honest and complete explanation, he is *not* a twister.

CHAPTER ELEVEN

YOUR HOMEWORK KIT

You can save yourself a lot of confusion if you will do some preliminary evaluation on your own. Ideally, you and your wife should work together on this so you both understand what is involved. Too many widows have suffered anguish and uncertainties because their husbands didn't consider it necessary to bring their wives into their planning. Also, wives sometimes refuse to become involved in family financial planning. Do your best to make this a joint project and decision.

This is not a book on financial planning, but you should not ignore how you are now spending the money you earn. You may be getting a better than average return for your dollars, but then again, you may not. Let's go through a simple exercise to see how your money usage checks out.

Most families have installment loans for purchases of cars, appliances, clothing, etc. These obligations frequently involve annual interest costs of 12% to 18%. Let's assume these are your current obligations:

Obligation	Amount Owed	Annual Rate of Interest
Department store	$ 400	18%
Credit card	$ 200	18%
Car loan	$1,000	12%
Personal loan	$ 300	12%
Total obligations	$1,900	

NOTE: The "Truth-in-Lending" law requires that you be advised of the annual interest rate you are being charged. If you are not certain, check with your creditor.

119

Next, let's assume your have these assets:

Asset	Amount	Annual Rate of Interest
Credit union	$ 500	6%
Bank savings account	$ 400	5%
Cash value of life insurance	$2,000	3% (approx.)

Are you getting the message? The $2,000 in your insurance policy is earning a magnificent 3% or thereabouts per year while you are paying interest costs of 12% and 18%! If you used this money to pay off your installment loans, you would be guaranteed an increase of 9% to 15% in the working power of your money! It's really more than this. An increase from 3% to 12% actually quadruples the effectiveness of your dollars.

If this strikes a nerve, review your own assets and obligations. If you end up with a similar picture, your first step is to get your money from the life insurance company. *You do not cancel the policy at this time.* Instead, you borrow the money for a while.

Borrowing the cash value does not terminate your coverage. The death benefit is reduced by the amount of your loan, but the remaining protection stays in force as long as you pay the premiums.

To get your money, send a letter to the home office of the insurance company reading as follows:

Gentlemen:
Reference policy #_____on the life of (name of insured person).

Please send all available cash values as a *loan* on this policy.

I also want to withdraw all accumulated dividends. (Include this sentence only if it is a participating policy).

If there are any forms for me to sign, please include them with your check.

Sincerely,
(Signature of policyowner).

You should receive a reply in about two weeks. The company can legally delay loaning you your money for six months. However, most companies are fairly prompt in processing requests for loans. You may first receive one of the formal loan request forms, even though you ask for the check and forms at the same time. If this happens, go along with their stalling game, complete the form and return it promptly. If you haven't received your money within two weeks after returning the form, write or call your state insurance department. This usually brings results.

NOTE: Do not send the policy with your request to borrow the money. The company may ask for it later, *but don't send it unless they ask for it.*

Whether you have an immediate need for the money or not, it is still a good idea to borrow the money as soon as you have decided to get new insurance. You will be charged interest of 5% or 6% from the date of the loan until you finally cancel the policy. You can offset this cost by investing the money where it will earn at least as much as you are paying.

Insurance companies have been known to make honest errors in computing loan and surrender values. This has happened more frequently when the transaction was handled by an agency other than the home office. So be sure to send your loan request to the home office, not the local agency.

By borrowing the money before you get new insurance, you determine the exact surrender value. If there are any discrepancies, you can detect them while you still have the policy in your possession. Later on, when you actually surrender the policy, you have to send the policy with your request.

In case you are still debating about keeping that precious, guaranteed cash-value policy that is going to send your youngsters through college, provide retirement income for you and your wife plus leaving all sorts of money for your children after you both pass on, your next step is to find out what this gem is really costing you. The Policy Analysis Worksheet will help you with this opera-

Policy Analysis Worksheet

Policy Number & Company	(1) Face Amount	(2) Cash Value	(3) Actual Insurance	(4) Annual Premium	(5) Latest Dividend	(6) 5% of Cash Value	(7) Total Cost	(8) Cost Per Thousand
Illustration								
Friendly Insurance #34 567 890	$10,000	$3,000	$7,000	$200	($70)	$150	$280	$40.00

tion. First, let's review the illustrated figures in this worksheet:

Column 1, Face Amount: In this column list only the death benefit of the basic policy. If your policy has a term rider or family coverage, these items should be listed separately.

Column 2, Cash Value: The policy's table of non-forfeiture values usually shows the amounts for each of the first twenty years and at ages 60 and 65. It is easier to use the nearest full year rather than to calculate intermediate values between anniversary dates. For example, if the issue date is July 1, 1968, and today's date is March 1, 1974, the nearest anniversary date would be July 1, 1974, when the policy would be six years old. Therefore, use the sixth-year cash value rather than computing a figure for five years and nine months.

Column 3, Actual Insurance: This is the difference between the face amount and the cash value. ($10,000 minus $3,000 equals $7,000).

Column 4, Annual Premium: This is the total amount of dollars of gross premium before allowance (if any) for dividends.

Column 5, Latest Dividend: You should have a statement from the company telling you how much of your money they refunded on the latest anniversary date of your policy.

Column 6, 5% of Cash Value: Multiply the amount in Col. 2 by .05. This is the amount of interest that your money could be earning at 5% if it were not locked up within the policy where each increase benefits the insurance company. It could also be the amount of interest you might be paying if you borrowed your cash value.

Column 7, Total Cost: This is the true cost of your insurance and is derived as follows:

Annual premium	$200
Less latest dividend	$(70)
Net premium	$130
Add 5% of cash value	$150
Total cost	$280

Column 8, Cost per Thousand: When you divide $280 by 7 (the number of thousands of protection), your answer is $40 per $1,000 of actual insurance.

BUT MY AGENT TOLD ME THAT NEXT YEAR'S INCREASE IN CASH VALUE WILL EQUAL MY PREMIUM AND THAT THE DIVIDEND WILL BE LARGER!

He may be right. Let's assume that he is and see what happens to your cost of protection.

Face amount	$10,000	(no change)
Less cash value	− 3,200	(increase of $200)
Actual insurance	$ 6,800	(decrease of $200)

(You are now supplying $200 more of your own death benefit than before!)

Annual premium	$ 200	(no change)
Less latest dividend	− 80	(increase of $10)
Net premium	$ 120	(decrease of $10)
Add 5% of cash value	+ 160	(increase of $10)
Total cost	$ 280	(no change)
Cost per Thousand	$41.18	(increase of $1.18)

The cost per thousand of protection has to increase each and every year because *you have less actual insurance and are losing a greater amount of interest each year.* It's as simple as that, and there is no way to avoid it if you insist on buying cash-value life insurance.

If your policy has a term rider, you may be a bit shocked when you compute the cost of insurance for this part of your policy and compare it with the base policy. Here are some figures from a recent case involving a $10,000 whole-life policy with a twenty-year decreasing term rider. The rider was originally $15,000, but had reduced to $6,900.

	Base Policy	Term Rider	Totals
Face amount	$10,000	$6,900	$16,900
Less cash value	− 1,690	——	− 1,690
Actual insurance	$ 8,310	$6,900	$15,210
Cost of protection			
Annual premium	$190.20	$41.40	$231.60
Less latest dividend	− 65.00	——	− 65.00
Net premium	$125.20	$41.40	$166.60
Add 5% of cash value*	+ 84.50	——	+ 84.50
Total cost	$209.70	$41.40	$251.10
Cost per thousand of protection	$ 25.23	$ 6.00	

This policy was the total insurance coverage of a thirty-nine-year-old father with a wife and three children. How long do you suppose this $16,900 would have lasted his family after his death?

Fortunately, he saw the light and bought $50,000 of decreasing term to age 65 for an annual premium of $239.50. This is only $7.90 more than he had been paying for an actual protection of $15,210 ($16,900 minus $1,690 of cash value equals $15,210). In addition, he now has this $1,690 earning 6% interest in his company's credit union. This provides $101.40 per year or almost half of his term insurance premium. The total of his old premium $231.50 and the interest of $101.50 is $333 per year. After paying his insurance premium of $239.50, he has $93.50 left. The important feature, however, is that his family now has *$50,000* of protection rather than *$16,900*.

This case illustrates another point. This man was saving $70 per week in his company's credit union. Who forced him to do this? It certainly does refute the claim of the life insurance industry that people have to be forced to save, doesn't it?

*Refer again to the explanation of the Policy Analysis Worksheet, Col. 6.

BUT AFTER AGE 65, HE WON'T
HAVE ANY INSURANCE!

He had been sold the whole life policy with the promise of money that he would get back. This policy would have had a guaranteed cash value of $6,000 at age 65. His $1,690 at 6% will grow to $7,253 from his age 39 to age 65. If he had kept the whole-life policy, he could have cashed it in at age 65, and would have received $6,000. Besides having no insurance, he would also have received $1,253 less in cash.

NOTE: The $7,253 is the ending value of a one time investment of $1,690 at 6 percent for 25 years. It does not include his annual savings of $93.50. This amount per year for 25 years would grow to $5,438. When combined with the $7,253, the total is $12,691 compared with the $6,000 of the old policy.

The next part of your homework kit is the Net Worth Worksheet. The purpose of this step is to determine the difference between what you own and what you owe. You are not actually going to convert everything to cash, pay off all your debts and then try to live on what you have left. However, your widow and orphans might be forced to do exactly this if you don't have enough life insurance and other assets to provide the money they need.

Be as realistic as possible in completing the Net Worth Worksheet. Money in cash and savings accounts is easy to list and has a definite value. However, if you took a flyer in Hoopty Scoop Electronics awhile back and the stock is now practically worthless, be honest and show it as zero value. Or you might have bought a Florida land scheme several years ago that was going to triple in value and put you on easy street (according to the salesman). Instead of tripling, you now find that you can't even sell it for what you paid for it. Since it has no market value, you would be better off to omit it from your list of assets.

If you loaned money to your brother-in-law five years ago and he has never made any attempts to repay you, don't list this as an asset. He is no more apt to repay your widow than you.

Your stamp collection may be priceless to you, but unless you can convert it to ready cash in a few days, omit it from your net worth figures. Place a reasonable value on your home and other real estate. Just because your neighbor said he sold a house like yours for $35,000 last year isn't sufficient reason to value yours at the same price. Don't go overboard on evaluating your business, either. It may be a money-maker for you, but of no value to anyone else as far as marketability is concerned. Shop around and see what kind of offers you can get.

NET WORTH WORKSHEET

ASSETS

Cash in checking accounts	$_____	
Savings accounts	$_____	
Stocks, bonds, mutual funds	$_____	
Cash value of life insurance	$_____	
Market value of home	$_____	
Market value of other real estate	$_____	
Market value of business	$_____	
Money owed to you	$_____	
Other assets	$_____	
TOTAL ASSETS		$_____

LIABILITIES

Mortage on home	$_____	
Mortgage on other real estate	$_____	
Charge accounts	$_____	
Auto loans	$_____	
Bank loans	$_____	
Other debts	$_____	_____
TOTAL LIABILITIES		$
NET WORTH		$_____

When you have completed the worksheet and determined your net worth, assume that you had this amount of money earning 6% per pear, or $5.00 per month per $1,000 invested. How much monthly income would this give you? Would this be enough to support you and your children?

THAT'S HARDLY A REASONABLE ASSUMPTION. I WOULD STILL HAVE MY JOB AND WOULD NOT BE COMPLETELY DEPENDENT UPON THIS MONEY FOR INCOME.

You are right—it is not a truly valid assumption. However, neither is it completely unreasonable. The fact that you would have a job is not the same as saying that your widow would be able to earn an equivalent amount of money. If she has to go to work, your children would be without a full-time mother. Working wives and working widows have quite different situations.

There is another consideration. If your widow earns more than a stated amount, she loses her portion of Social Security benefits—if you are covered by Social Security.

When you have completed the Net Worth Worksheet, keep it on file and review it from time to time to find out if you are moving forward, backward or standing still.

If you operate on a budget, the next step—Money Needs Per Month—can be completed more easily than if you just spend what you have without much concern as to where it is going. Get out your bills and checkbook so that you can record actual costs involved, not just estimates.

In more cases than not, it works out that the survivors will need about 70% of what you are now spending in order to maintain the same standard of living. How does it work out for you?

The Life Insurance Worksheet is next; let's go over each item:

1. Monthly income needed by family: If you have completed the Money Needs Per Month worksheet, put this figure in this space. If not, use 70% of your present expenditures.

2. Social Security or other benefits: In most cases, a substantial portion of your family's income will be supplied by Social Security. As long as any of your children are under age 18, both your widow and orphans will be eligible for Social Security. When your youngest reaches age

18, the widow's portion stops until she reaches age 60. If your children are full-time students, they will receive Social Security until age 22.

Social Security survivor benefits vary considerably with the husband's age at time of death, number of working years, average monthly income, number of survivors, etc. These are constantly being changed, and any figures listed now would probably be outdated by the time you read

MONEY NEEDS PER MONTH

	Present Amounts	Survivors' Amounts
Rent or mortgage payments	$_____	$_____
Utilities	_____	_____
Food and household supplies	_____	_____
Medical and dental expenses	_____	_____
Car insurance premiums	_____	_____
Car expenses	_____	_____
Home insurance	_____	_____
Home maintenance expenses	_____	_____
Property taxes	_____	_____
Clothing, laundry and dry cleaning	_____	_____
Household help	_____	_____
Recreation	_____	_____
Education	_____	_____
Installment payments	_____	_____
Life insurance premiums	_____	_____
Disability insurance premiums	_____	_____
Medical insurance premiums	_____	_____
Additions to savings or investments	_____	_____
Vacations	_____	_____
Churches, charities and other contributions	_____	_____
Other needs (list)	_____	_____
_____	_____	_____
_____	_____	_____
TOTALS PER MONTH	$_____	$_____

this. Your best choice is to contact the nearest Social Security Office. Remember, that if your widow works and earns more than a given amount, her benefits are reduced or terminated.

"Other benefits" might include pension plans from your employer, military or federal civil service survivor plans, veterans' benefits, etc.

3. *Additional income needed:* The difference between items 1 and 2.

4. *Lump sum needed to supply this income:* Money invested at 6% will supply an income of $5.00 per month per $1,000 invested. If item 3 shows a need for an additional $300 per month, your widow would need $60,000 invested at 6% to produce this income. The quick way to determine the lump sum needed is to multiply the monthly income figure by 200. ($300 x 200 equals $60,000). This may seem like a tremendous amount of money, but remember that your widow will still need income from the time your youngest reaches age 18 until she reaches age 60. She may remarry or go to work, but you cannot assume that she will.

NOTE: Also keep in mind that you are thinking of today's prices. Inflation, in varying degrees, is here to stay and it would be completely unrealistic to assume that living costs are going to decrease.

5. *Mortgage and other large debts:* Your widow may decide not to pay off the mortgage on your home. In some cases, a paid-for home is an advantage; in others, it's a disadvantage. The main thought to keep in mind is to be sure that she either has the cash to pay off the mortgage or the income to keep up the payments. If you want her to make the payments, include this amount in Item 1. If you want her to pay off the loan, include the loan balance in item 5.

NOTE: Do you have credit life insurance on your installment loans? If so, these debts should be excluded from this item.

6. *Children's college fund:* You can estimate a minimum of $3,000 per year per child for college costs. This is an

optional item. You may conclude that if your youngster wants additional education after high school badly enough, he will find a way to get it. Alternately, you may want to be certain that there will be money for college when needed. It's your choice.

7. *Final expenses:* Medical, burial, legal and similar expenses can eat up a lot of dollars. *The Widow's Study* showed average final expenses of $3,900. The actual figures will vary with the length of sickness before death, type of hospital and medical insurance you have, complexity of your estate, and other factors. Try to be as realistic as possible.

8. *Reserve fund:* A recommended figure is 12 times Item 1, equal to one year's income. Increase this if you like, but do not decrease it.

The transition from wife to widow is loaded with extra and unanticipated expenses. Appliances seem to break down more often when the man of the house isn't around; your widow may have to move to another part of the country; she will probably need a new car; there may be unexpected medical or dental bills. You can probably think of other possible costs.

9. *Family's total needs:* Don't get panicky if this amount is well over $100,000.

10. *Present savings and investments:* Include only assets that are easily salable and that can produce income. Exclude that Florida land and similar questionable "assets."

11. *Face value of present life insurance:* Include all personal insurance. Group insurance should be included only if you are absolutely certain that you will continue with your present employer until retirement age and that you will always have at least the amount of group life insurance you now have. Individual term insurance coverage is so inexpensive that you should be able to afford the premiums and thus eliminate relying upon group coverage that might end at a most inopportune time.

12. *Amount of insurance to be added or dropped:* Are you over- or under-insured?

NOTE: Many families complain about being "insurance

poor." This is seldom true. What they mean is that they are "premium poor" because they are overpaying for what they have. Have you ever heard of a widow complaining that her husband had too much life insurance?

LIFE INSURANCE WORKSHEET

1. Monthly income needed by your family $_____
2. Subtract Social Security or other benefits — _____
3. Additional income needed $_____
4. Lump sum needed to supply this income _____
5. Mortgage and other large debts _____
6. Children's college fund _____
7. Total of items 4, 5 & 6 _____
8. Final expenses $_____
9. Reserve fund _____
10. Family's total needs _____
11. Subtract present savings & investments _____
12. Family's net needs $_____
13. Face value of present life insurance _____
14. Amount of life insurance to be added or dropped $_____

Now turn to the Appendix and review the sample premiums for various forms of term insurance. How much honest protection can you buy with your present premium? Will this be more or less than the amount in Item 14 of your worksheet? If you buy the amount in Item 14, will your total premiums increase or decrease?

BUT IF I DROP MY PRESENT INSURANCE AND BUY NEW INSURANCE, I WILL LOSE ALL THE MONEY I'VE PAID IN!

You will lose even more if you keep your present insurance, to say nothing of the fact that you are probably underprotecting your family and overpaying for protection. Here is how to figure the cost of keeping your present cash-value insurance.

Let's forget about your present premium for the moment and think about your present cash value only. To keep it simple, let's assume you now have $1,000 of cash value ambling along at 3%. (The interest rate on your policy may be less than 3%; check and see). If this $1,000 were to be invested at a conservative 5%, here is what would happen:

Number of Years	Value at 3%	Value at 5%	Dollar Difference	Percentile Difference
5	$1,159	$1,276	$ 117	10% more
10	1,344	1,629	285	21% more
15	1,558	2,079	521	33% more
20	1,806	2,653	847	47% more
25	2,094	3,386	1,292	62% more
30	2,427	4,322	1,895	78% more
35	2,814	5,516	2,702	96% more

Keep in mind that this is your present cash value only. Do not confuse the above values with the amounts for future years given in your policy. These policy figures include additions from future premiums; the above figures do not. Isn't it amazing what a difference of 2% per year can amount to?

It's quite possible that you should continue to spend as much for life insurance as you are now paying. Most families are sadly underprotected, because they have been misled about life insurance. However, let's assume that you now have adequate insurance, but are overpaying. As an illustration, let's say that new term insurance will cost you $1,000 less per year than at present. If you put this money to work at 5%, this is what it will grow to:

Number of Years	Value at 5%
5	$ 5,802
10	13,207
15	22,658
20	34,719
25	50,114
30	69,761
35	94,836

The Appendix includes two compound interest tables. One is identified as "Accumulation of One Dollar Principle" and gives the values of a one-time lump sum investment for one to forty years at various rates of interest. The second one is headed "Accumulation of One Dollar Deposited at the Beginning of Each Year." If you believe the 5% is too conservative, select a different interest rate and for the desired period of time. All you need to do is to multiply the factor for one dollar by the amount of your investment.

CHAPTER TWELVE

SOME DO'S AND DON'TS

It's quite probable that much of this information is new to you and needs to be summarized and reviewed. Here are some key points to keep in mind:

1. DO NOT compromise your family's welfare! If your worksheet shows that you need $100,000 or $200,000 of life insurance—don't hedge. Buy the full amount that your calculations show you need. The premium may be more than you are now paying, but don't fudge and jeopardize your family's financial security. If you are now paying $200 per year for $15,000 of cash-value insurance and your worksheet shows that you should have $50,000 of protection—buy the $50,000. Don't shortchange your family by buying just $15,000 of term insurance so that you can save the difference in premium. It takes a long time to accumulate $35,000—the difference in coverage.

2. DO decide on what type of term insurance best fits your situation, either level or decreasing. If you choose decreasing term, your premium will remain the same for the life of the policy and the amount of protection will reduce. Straight-line reducing term is a good buy as long as you realize that it decreases more rapidly than the "in-between" or mortgage term. If you prefer level coverage along with the ability to control the amount of protection, your choice should be renewable and convertible level term.

3. DO NOT buy "short-term." Buy coverage that you can keep in force to at least age 65. If you are now age 30, for instance, do not buy twenty-year term as your entire program just because you now believe that you won't need insurance after age 50. Your guess may be right, but

if you are wrong and still need insurance after age 50, you may be in trouble. Your health could deteriorate to the point that you can't buy insurance at any price. If not insurable at standard rates, you might have to pay an extra charge for "rated" insurance. Or you might be forced to convert your low-cost term protection to higher-cost permanent insurance if you can't afford to be without insurance. If your guess is correct and you no longer need insurance at age 50, just drop the term policy. It's much better that you have it and not need it than to need it and not be able to get it.

NOTE: Insurance salesmen have been known to sell "short-term" so that you can be more easily persuaded to convert to high-cost permanent insurance at a later date. "Second sale—second (and higher) commission" is the name of the game. Don't fall for this bait. Insist that at least a portion of your term insurance can be continued to age 65 or 70. You might even want to buy some decreasing term to age 100. Some companies sell this as a base plan with a term rider to age 65 or 70.

4. DO consider making your wife the owner of your insurance policy in order to avoid estate taxes on the proceeds. If you are the owner, the death proceeds are included in your taxable estate. If your wife (or some other adult or your company) is the owner, the proceeds are not included in your taxable estate.

Only the policyowner can make any changes in the policy or exercise options such as conversion rights. In the case of permanent insurance, your wife as owner could surrender the policy whenever she wanted to. However, term insurance is protection only, has little or no cash surrender value, and you need not be concerned about this possibility. Your wife as owner could change beneficiaries from your children to someone else she selects. If you are worried about this possibility, designate someone else as the owner or make yourself the owner, in which case the policy will be part of your taxable estate.

5. DO specify whom you want as beneficiary in case of your death. Your wife will probably be the primary one. In case of her death, your children will most likely be the

secondary beneficiaries. If this is your wish, the beneficiary designation should read as follows:

> "To my wife, Mary Jane Doe, if living; otherwise to all children of this marriage, share and share alike."

It is not advisable to list each child individually. If you now have two children and list them by name as secondary beneficiaries and then acquire more children at a later date, the newcomers would be disinherited if you forgot to change the beneficiary designation.

Also avoid naming your estate as the beneficiary. If the estate is named as beneficiary, the proceeds will be included in your taxable estate and will be subject to unnecessary legal and probate fees.

6. DO consider the idea of establishing a life insurance trust. Your attorney or trust department of your bank can advise you on procedures, advantages and disadvantages.

7. DO include waiver of premium coverage when you buy your term insurance. This provides for keeping your insurance in force if you are disabled for more than six months. Some companies offer waiver of premium that not only pays the term premiums while you are disabled, but also provides for automatic conversion to permanent insurance if you are still disabled at age 60. The company continues to pay the permanent insurance premiums for as long as you are disabled. This could be a tremendous benefit if you were involved in an accident that left you paralyzed for life. Accident victims sometimes survive for many years.

8. DO NOT assume that you will die an accidental death. It is possible, but don't pin your family's welfare on this possibility. Buy the amount of life insurance that your survivors will need, regardless of how you might die. If you need $100,000 of protection, don't buy $50,000 of life insurance plus $50,000 of accidental death benefit on the assumption that your family would be certain to receive $100,000. If you die from a heart attack or from the effects of surgery, the accidental death coverage would not pay off.

9. DO buy insurance on your wife. You can get a term

rider on your policy or a separate term policy on her alone. Another choice might be "joint life." This is a single policy insuring both husband and wife for the same amount. The premium is less than for two individual policies, and you can buy joint life term insurance. Ask the salesman about it. This is a good choice when your wife is bringing home a goodly portion of the family income.

10. DO NOT buy insurance on your children just because the premiums are low. You may want to add a child insurance rider to your term policy, but don't let yourself be conned into buying permanent insurance to "give the little ones a head start on their insurance program," as a recent commercial advises.

11. DO NOT withhold any pertinent information about your health or personal activities when you apply for insurance. If you are taking flying lessons, for example, say so. If you conceal this information and then spin in, your family gets your premiums back—and that's all. Be completely honest and be certain that the salesman and medical examiner records all that you tell them. Remember the discussion of the contestable period?

12. DO NOT be too proud to admit that you were sold a bill of goods when you signed up for cash values and dividends. You probably will not be able to recoup all your past premiums. Whatever your "loss" may be, you can be quite certain that you will lose even more by holding onto your "sacred" permanent insurance. What is more important is the possible loss to your family. Your false pride and reluctance to admit that you made a bad buy won't put much food on the table for your widow and children.

13. DO NOT let the salesman talk you into buying cash value insurance. If he insists on extolling the virtues of permanent insurance or downgrades the idea of true protection term insurance, thank him for his time and call another salesman who will sell you what you need and want.

NOTE: You should have less trouble in locating a term insurance salesman now than a few years ago. According to the 1973 *Life Insurance Fact Book*, about 41% of new insurance purchased in 1972 was term insurance.

14. DO NOT cancel your present policies until you have your new policy in your possession and have paid the first premium. Signing an application and taking a physical does not automatically insure you.

15. DO borrow your present cash values and withdraw any accumulated dividends as soon as you have decided that term insurance is what you want.

16. DO compare the costs of paying your premium on an annual basis versus semiannual, quarterly, or monthly. Most companies offer an automatic check plan through your checking account. There is usually an extra charge for this convenience, so ask the salesman to explain the difference.

17. DO NOT delay your decision! You are probably underprotecting your family or overpaying for protection or otherwise misusing your money.

18. DO remember that you are now a buyer—not just someone being sold something!

CHAPTER THIRTEEN

SOME FINAL THOUGHTS

The various features of life insurance discussed herein are the results of the questions I have been asked many times during several years of selling the benefits of term life insurance. (At times I felt I should have a teaching certificate rather than a salesman's license.) The questions came from factory workers, executives, professional persons, people with varying levels of income and formal education. (Almost everyone seems to be confused about life insurance.)

There is a certain amount of repetition throughout the book. This is intentional. As a result of countless personal interviews and discussions, I have found that repetition is necessary to overcome the brainwashing of the life insurance industry that we have been subjected to for so many years. I realize that it is difficult to change the beliefs of a lifetime. I had to *myself!* I paid premiums for fourteen years on a twenty-payment life policy before I found out how to buy insurance wholesale. In my case, I was paying $300 per year for $8,000 of protection bought at age 27. Fortunately for my family, I didn't die before I discovered the value of term insurance.

If you doubt what I have said or want more specific information that is beyond the scope of this book, here are some suggested sources of information:

1. Capital Planning Corporation, 34 Oak Terrace, P.O. Box 13152 St. Louis, Mo. 63119
2. Mutual Fund Services, 180 Church St., Naugatuck, Connecticut 06770
3. Dr. Laurence Curly, P.O. Box 17635, Tucson, Arizona 85710

All of these sources stock a wide variety of literature explaining the disadvantages of cash value insurance and the benefits of term insurance. Write and ask for their catalogs.

An informative and well-documented reference is *What's Wrong With Your Life Insurance?* by Norman F. Dacey, published by Collier, MacMillan. This is now in paperback and can be purchased at most bookstores for $1.50.

You might also want to read *The Mortality Merchants* by G. Scott Reynolds. (David McKay Company, Inc., N.Y.) This is a hardcover that sells for $6.95.

Consumers Union, Orangeburg, N.Y. 10962 offers *The Consumers Union Report on Life Insurance* for $2.00 to non-subscribers and $1.50 to subscribers.

Discuss what you have learned about life insurance with your friends, relatives and neighbors. They probably have as many unanswered questions about life insurance as you did.

Be especially sure that your children are told how to buy life insurance. An excellent wedding gift is a low-cost term policy. Pay the first annual premium yourself and then let them take over as soon as they are able. It may help you pay for raising your grandchildren.

If you believe that an insurance plan is or was misrepresented to you, report the circumstances to your state insurance department. The advertising and selling techniques of the life insurance industry are being scrutinized by several states. Some states have prepared guides for insurance buyers; others have installed toll-free "hot lines" to answer consumers' questions. Check with your state insurance department to see what they have to offer.

Let your legislators know of your concern about how life insurance is presented and sold. They can't help you unless you tell them. The life insurance industry is state-regulated only. Possibly some form of federal control will be considered necessary if state regulation alone doesn't do the job. We now have a federal "truth-in-lending" law. A federal "truth-in-insurance" law could be next.

NOTE: Can you imagine the plight of the cash-value insurance salesman if he were required to explain and justify a 70%-80% first-year sales charge for permanent insurance?

The life insurance lobby is powerful and well financed (with your money). The companies have been able to disguise themselves as great benefactors of mankind, interested only in you—the insurance-buying public. However, they are having to recognize that this is the era of "Naderism" and that the interest in consumers and consumerism may curtail some of their past practices. They are finally realizing the public's negative attitude toward life insurance and are spending more and more of your money to correct this image. In December 1973, the Institute of Life Insurance and the Health Insurance Institute proposed a five-million-dollar advertising campaign designed to:

> "1. Help consumers better evaluate life and health insurance, thus making them more knowledgeable buyers.
>
> 2. Demonstrate that the life and health insurance industries are working hard in the best interests of all Americans; that they are delivering services essential to the nation; and that the companies making up these industries are competitive, delivering good products at fair prices."*

Although the idea of the companies spending your money to correct their mistakes and to improve their public image isn't the tastiest plan ever offered, it is somewhat satisfying to know that they are aware of their shortcomings. Several other industries have already been rocked by the efforts of the consumer forces, and the life insurance industry would like to avoid being *legislated* into giving the public a fair deal. If they can convince you that they are sincerely concerned about the welfare of you and your family, they can probably continue to get away with some of their questionable methods. So be on guard for some more propaganda from the "Do No Wrong" life insurance industry. You should now have enough information to be a knowledgeable buyer of pure protection term life insurance.

*The National Underwriter, Life & Health Edition, December 1, 1973.

EPILOGUE

The Pension Reform Act of 1974 has set the stage for another monstrous ripoff of John Q Public by the life insurance industry!

This important legislation made drastic changes in the administration of corporate pension plans, many of which were very unfair to employees. This law also added a brand new item—Individual Retirement Account (IRA). It's the IRA that has the life insurance industry licking its chops in glee as it contemplates all the easy money that (they hope) will be coming into their coffers.

Briefly, the IRA program permits any worker who is not covered by a private or governmental retirement plan to establish his own personal program. An eligible worker can put up to 15% of his compensation into an IRA plan with the maximum amount per year being $1,500. His contribution may be deducted from his income and the dividends and/or interest his money earns is tax sheltered until he withdraws it, usually after age 59½.

You can put your IRA money into savings accounts, special government bonds, mutual funds, common trust funds and certain life insurance plans. It's these "certain life insurance plans" that you need to know about.

The law specifically prohibits putting IRA money into whole life and limited payment plans such as 20 payment life and life paid up at age 65. Instead, the law specifically authorizes endowment plans and annuities.

NOTE: The general classification of "endowment plans" includes "income endowments," more commonly known as Retirement Income Insurance. Retirement income insurance is sold in units to provide increments of $10 per month of retired pay and includes a death benefit of $1,000 per $10 unit. You should realize that these are the biggest moneymakers of all life insurance products—

for the companies, not you. They also entail the least amount of risk against premature death because the premium is many times the pure mortality risk. These plans also provide that when the cash value exceeds the face value, the death benefit is equal to the cash value.

To illustrate, let's examine a typical Retirement Income Insurance at Age 65 for a male age 35. The annual premium is $36 which provides an initial death benefit of $1,000 and a cash value at age 65 of $1,582. This $1,582, in turn, will provide a lifetime income of $10 per month, starting at age 65. Here is how this gem would progress from age 35 to 65:

End of Year	Total Premium	Cash Value	Death Benefit
1	$ 36	$ 0.00	$1,000
2	72	22.80	1,000
3	108	56.18	1,000
4	144	90.63	1,000
5	180	126.17	1,000
6	216	162.83	1,000
7	252	200.66	1,000
8	288	239.70	1,000
9	324	280.02	1,000
10	360	321.67	1,000
11	396	364.70	1,000
12	432	409.20	1,000
13	468	455.22	1,000
14	504	502.87	1,000
15	540	552.24	1,000
16	576	603.44	1,000
17	612	656.61	1,000
18	648	711.92	1,000
19	684	769.54	1,000
20	720	829.68	1,000
25	900	1,172.49	1,172.49
30 (Age 65)	1,080	1,582.00	1,582

If you haven't already, please note these items:

1. No first year cash value. A 35 year old can buy honest death protection for about $3.00 per $1000. What happened to the other $33?

2. A guaranteed loss for practically 15 years. Total premiums: $540; cash value: $552.24 for a grand gain of $12.24. Do you understand why the life insurance companies love to sell retirement income plans?

3. The cash value exceeds the face value in about 22 years. From this point on, you would be completely self insured and the company would have absolutely no risk left.

4. A "profit" of $402 after 30 years. If your $36 per year earned only 3%, you would end up with $1,677. If invested at 6%, your ending value would be $2,810 or $1,228 more!

The second type of plan authorized by the IRA legislation is the Retirement Income Annuity. This is similar to the Retirement Income Insurance in that it is designed to provide units of $10 per month at retirement. However, it contains no insurance element. It is simply a savings program sponsored by a life insurance company. The death benefit is equal to the total premiums paid or the cash value, whichever is greater.

Again using age 35 as an illustration, the premium per $10 of retirement income at age 65 would be $33.72 per year. Here is how your money would charge along over 30 years:

End of Year	Total Premium	Cash Value
1	$ 33.72	$ 16.86
2	67.44	48.86
3	101.16	81.98
4	134.88	116.26
5	168.60	151.74
6	202.32	188.46
7	236.04	226.47
8	269.76	265.80
9	303.48	306.51
10	337.20	348.65

End of Year	Total Premium	Cash Value
11	370.92	392.27
12	404.64	437.41
13	438.36	484.13
14	472.08	532.48
15	505.80	579.15
16	539.52	634.33
17	573.24	687.94
18	606.96	743.42
19	640.68	800.89
20	674.40	860.30
25	843.00	1,190.20
30 (Age 65)	1,011.60	1,582.00

Please make note of these features:

1. First year sales charge of 50%. Do you know of any bank or savings and loan that would take half of your first year's deposit?

2. Nine year break-even point. If you wanted to quit after the ninth year, you could surrender the plan for a wonderful profit of $3.03.

3. A bare 3% per year return for your money after 30 years. Your $33.72 in Series E bonds at 6% would be worth $2,825.74 which is $1,243.74 more than this retirement income annuity would provide.

Both plans illustrated are non-par plans of a major stock company. Plans offered by the mutual companies will promise dividends to try to persuade you to give your IRA money to them. Don't fall for their pitch!

The premiums for participatng retirement plans are about 25% higher than the non-par plan illustrated here. At age 35, the typical premium for Retirement Income Insurance is around $45, or $9.00 more than the typical non-par.

If you are approached to buy an IRA from an insurance agent, insist that he provide the same breakdown for his plan as provided here. Don't let him bamboozle you into buying simply by showing you a single cash value figure for age 65 or only a single amount of monthly income at age 65. Insist on a year by year illustration so that you know how much it is front loaded and what kind of over-all results you will get. To repeat, be especially mistrustful of all participating plans!

It's possible that some companies will design and sell plans that will give a buyer a decent return for his money. Therefore, don't completely close the door.

If you find a good-paying annuity, buy that in preference to retirement income insurance. The taxes that you save by investing in an IRA will buy a bunch of term life insurance.

APPENDIX

It would be a confusing mess of figures and data to try to list all the life insurance plans of the roughly 1,800 companies in business today. It would also be a completely useless collection of information. The variety of titles alone would fill a small encyclopedia. You would still have the problem of trying to differentiate between "The President's Plan," "The Accumulator," "High Value L 65," "Life Multiplier" to name a few of the tricky designations used by the life insurance companies.

The tables of typical premiums are identified with the same descriptions that were used in the text and you should have no trouble in deciding whether a plan is level or decreasing term or a level or decreasing premium. Insofar as possible, the premiums listed are among the best available. They are not guaranteed to be the lowest in the country, but all are considered "Good Buys" in their particular category.

Before getting into an explanation of the individual tables, there are a few points to be aware of:

1. Life insurance is cheaper by the dozen or more specifically by the thousands. The larger the policy, the lower the premium per $1,000. Most companies charge the highest premium for policies of $25,000 or less, a slightly lower premium for policies of $25,000 to $49,999, and an even lower premium for policies of $50,000 or more. Many companies offer policies in which the minimum face amount is $100,000 or $250,000. These discounted premiums apply to term as well as permanent plans. For example, Occidental Life of California charges $3.61 per 1000 for $25,000 of thirty-year straight-line decreasing term (age 35), but only $3.29 per 1000 for $50,000 or more.

2. A large number of companies use a policy fee in computing the total premium. This stated amount is also a form of discount that can be explained by comparing policies of different face amounts:

Face amount	$50,000	$100,000	$150,000
Life premium @ $3.29/1000	164.50	329.00	493.50
Policy fee	15.00	15.00	15.00
Total annual premium	$179.50	$ 344.00	$ 508.50
Average cost per $1,000	$ 3.59	$ 3.44	$ 3.39

As the policy size increases, the average cost per 1000 decreases.

3. In most companies you will save money if you pay the premiums on an annual basis. If you pay semiannually, quarterly, monthly or by bank draft, you will be charged an extra amount to cover the additional billing and administrative costs. The most costly mode of payment is when you are billed each month. A better mode is the bank draft or preauthorized check plan that most companies offer. This requires the completion of a simple form in which you authorize the insurance company to write a check for the amount of the premium on your checking account each month. The form also authorizes your bank to honor the check. This involves a little bookkeeping on your part since you have to be sure to deduct the amount from your checking account each month.

4. Your "insurance age" is not the same with all companies. The majority use "nearest birthday" meaning within six months of your birthday. Other companies use "last birthday" which means your present age. If you apply for insurance just after an age change, you can ask to have the policy backdated so that your premium will be based on the younger age. Ask the salesman to show the premiums for both ages. There may be only a slight difference, but it may be worth your while to ask.

5. Women can usually buy insurance for a lesser premium than men of the same age. Most companies have a three-year setback, meaning that a woman age 35 is

charged the premium for a man age 32. The Appendix tables are for men; for women, subtract three years.

Now for the Appendix tables.

Table I is for informational purposes to illustrate the amount of overcharge in a typical participating whole-life premium. The par premiums are those of a mutual company; the non-par premiums are those of a stock company. Neither are the highest or lowest in their category; they are simply typical.

Table II gives the annual premium for three different level-premium level-term plans available from Georgia International Life, P.O. Box 7325, Atlanta, Ga. 30309. This is one of the few companies offering level term to age 75. Premiums are based on last birthday, and the annual policy fee is $15.00

Table III lists the annual premiums for three different renewable and convertible level term plans of Old Line Life, 707 N. 11th St., Milwaukee, Wis. 53233. All three plans are renewable to age 70. This company uses last birthday, the annual policy fee is $10.00 and their monthly bank draft premium is one-twelfth of the annual premium. It is one of the few companies that does not charge extra for monthly bank draft. Note: The Pennsylvania Insurance Department prepared "A Shopper's Guide to Term Life Insurance" which compared the 5 year renewable and convertible term plans of 380 different companies. Old Line came out lowest overall.

Table IV lists the annual premiums, first-year deposit, tenth-year refund and average annual cost per $1,000 for the deposit term plan of University Life, P.O. Box 68192 Indianapolis, Ind. 46268. Premiums are based on nearest birthday, and this plan has no policy fee. Refer to the text for a discussion of deposit term.

Table V gives Old Line Life's rates for decreasing term to age 65, 70 and 100.

Table VI lists the straight-line decreasing term plans of Occidental Life of California, P.O. Box 2101, Terminal Annex, Los Angeles, Calif. 90051. All of these plans level off at 20% of the initial amount. This company uses nearest

150

birthday, has a $15.00 policy fee, and offers discounts large policies. The premiums listed here are for policies $25,000 to $49,999.

Table VII may need some clarification. "In-between" decreasing term reduces faster than mortgage term, but more gradually than straight-line. (See tables IX, X, XI and XII for a comparison). The rates listed are those of Old Line Life. Policy fee is $10.00 and premiums are based on last birthday.

Table VIII gives the premiums for Georgia International's mortgage cancellation decreasing term based on a 7½% mortgage. This company offers plans of ten to thirty years at one-year intervals. If your mortgage has only twenty-two years left, for example, you can buy twenty-two-year mortgage term. Policy fee is $15.00, and rates are based on last birthday.

NOTE: Contrary to what you may have been led to believe, you do not have to have a mortgage to buy mortgage term. If you prefer the gradual decrease of a mortgage term plan over the more rapid decrease of other decreasing term plans, mortgage term would be a sound choice.

Tables IX through XII compare the different rates of decrease for Occidental's straight-line term, Old Line's in-between term and Georgia International's 7½% mortgage term. You will note that there is a considerable difference in coverage in later years. For example, the thirty-year straight-line term reduces to 50% at the end of 15 years, the in-between to 60.9%, and the mortgage term to only 75.5%.

Obviously, no single form of decreasing term will fit all requirements. If you want the maximum *initial* protection per dollar outlay, straight-line term is your best choice. If you want a *more gradual reduction in coverage,* the mortgage term is the answer. If you want some of both features, a compromise could be the in-between term.

Let's say that you have decided that you can spend $300 per year for life insurance and that you are age 35. Here is what your $300 per year will buy:

151

Company and Type	Initial Amount	Annual Premium
Occidental 30-year straight-line term	$87,000	$301.23
Old Line 30-year in-between term	74,000	300.08
Georgia International 30-year mortgage term	54,000	303.90

As far as initial amount is concerned, the straight-line term plan would provide the most coverage and the mortgage plan the least. Here is how they would compare in later years:

Start of Year	30-Yr. Straight-Line Term	30-Yr. In-Between Term	30-Yr. Mortgage Term
1	$87,000	$74,000	$54,000
5	75,429	67,488	51,786
10	60,900	58,164	47,898
15	46,371	47,434	42,174
20	31,929	34,928	33,912
25	17,400	20,424	21,870
30	17,400	13,700	10,800

The above comparison is based on a given dollar outlay per year, and you have therefore probably concluded that straight-line term is the best buy. No argument—just a word of caution. Don't buy $30,000 of straight-line term to cover a thirty-year $30,000 mortgage, because the insurance coverage will drop much faster than your mortgage. You will need to buy a larger initial amount, and the exact amount will depend upon the interest rate and time period of your mortgage. Check the amortization schedule of your mortgage. If you don't have a schedule, ask your loan company for a copy.

You should now have a good idea of how inexpensively pure protection term insurance can be purchased. You have the knowledge and tools (worksheets) along with the names and home office addresses of a few Best Recommended companies that offer better than average rates. To repeat, the rates are not guaranteed to be the lowest in the country. If you find better values and your investigation satisfies you that the company is sound, don't hesitate to buy from them. Just because a company is not specifically mentioned here is no reason for you to refuse to do business with them.

TABLE I

Comparative Annual Whole Life Premiums (Par and Non-par)

Issue Age	Whole Life (Par)	Whole Life (Non-par)	Amount of Overcharge	Percentage Overcharge
20	$15.24	$10.20	$5.04	49%
21	15.63	10.52	5.11	49%
22	16.04	10.88	5.16	47%
23	16.44	11.25	5.19	46%
24	16.91	11.65	5.26	45%
25	17.37	12.06	5.31	44%
26	17.86	12.49	5.37	43%
27	18.36	12.94	5.42	42%
28	18.89	13.42	5.47	41%
29	19.44	13.92	5.52	40%
30	20.02	14.45	5.57	39%
31	20.62	15.01	5.61	37%
32	21.25	15.59	5.66	36%
33	21.91	16.21	5.70	35%
34	22.61	16.86	5.75	34%
35	23.34	17.55	5.79	33%
36	24.11	18.27	5.84	32%
37	24.91	19.04	5.87	31%
38	25.76	19.84	5.92	30%
39	26.65	20.68	5.97	29%
40	27.58	21.57	6.01	28%
41	28.56	22.46	6.10	27%
42	29.59	23.39	6.20	27%
43	30.67	24.38	6.29	26%
44	31.81	25.40	6.41	25%
45	33.01	26.44	6.57	25%
46	34.27	27.52	6.75	25%
47	35.60	28.70	6.90	24%
48	37.00	29.93	7.07	24%
49	38.48	31.20	7.28	23%
50	40.05	32.61	7.44	23%
51	41.70	34.22	7.48	22%
52	43.44	35.92	7.52	21%
53	45.28	37.73	7.55	20%
54	47.23	39.63	7.60	19%
55	49.30	41.66	7.64	18%
56	51.49	43.80	7.69	18%
57	53.82	46.08	7.74	17%
58	56.29	48.49	7.80	16%
59	58.90	51.05	7.85	15%
60	61.69	53.77	7.92	15%

"TYPICAL"

GEORGIA INT'L
TABLE II
Typical Level Premium—Level Coverage Term Plans
(Annual Premiums $1,000)

Issue Age	Level Term to Age 75	Level Term to Age 65	20-Year Level Term
20	$	$ 5.54	$ 3.03
21		5.69	3.10
22		5.83	3.17
23		5.98	3.24
24		6.15	3.34
25		6.35	3.45
26		6.57	3.57
27		6.82	3.71
28		7.08	3.86
29		7.36	4.04
30	11.27	7.65	4.26
31	11.75	7.96	4.50
32	12.26	8.28	4.76
33	12.80	8.62	5.05
34	13.37	8.98	5.40
35	13.97	9.36	5.83
36	14.60	9.76	6.34
37	15.27	10.18	6.91
38	15.96	10.61	7.54
39	16.69	11.06	8.25
40	17.44	11.52	9.03
41	18.23	11.99	9.88
42	19.06	12.48	10.80
43	19.92	12.99	11.79
44	20.78	13.49	12.85
45	21.62	14.00	14.00
46	22.42	14.48	15.20
47	23.20	14.94	16.46
48	23.99	15.41	17.80
49	24.81	15.94	19.27
50	25.72	16.58	20.90
51	26.71	17.34	22.67
52	27.75	18.19	24.58
53	28.85	19.10	26.63
54	29.99	20.05	28.83
55	31.17	21.00	
56	32.39	21.97	
57	33.65	22.96	
58	34.96	23.96	
59	36.30	24.99	
60	37.67		

OLD LINE LIFE A

TABLE III
Typical Renewable and Convertible Level Term Plans
(Annual Premiums/$1,000)

Issue Age	One-Year Ren. & Conv. Level Term	Five-Year Ren. & Conv. Level Term	Ten-Year Ren. & Conv. Level Term
20	$ 2.09	$ 2.10	$ 2.30
21	2.11	2.12	2.32
22	2.13	2.14	2.34
23	2.15	2.16	2.36
24	2.17	2.18	2.38
25	2.19	2.21	2.40
26	2.21	2.24	2.42
27	2.23	2.27	2.44
28	2.25	2.31	2.47
29	2.27	2.37	2.51
30	2.29	2.45	2.58
31	2.31	2.55	2.68
32	2.34	2.67	2.80
33	2.37	2.80	2.94
34	2.41	2.94	3.11
35	2.46	3.09	3.32
36	2.54	3.25	3.58
37	2.65	3.44	3.87
38	2.80	3.66	4.21
39	2.99	3.93	4.58
40	3.22	4.25	5.01
41	3.48	4.62	5.48
42	3.77	5.04	5.98
43	4.10	5.52	6.52
44	4.48	6.06	7.12
45	4.95	6.62	7.79
46	5.49	7.20	8.48
47	6.09	7.80	9.20
48	6.75	8.44	9.99
49	7.46	9.15	10.88
50	8.20	9.94	11.91
51	8.98	10.81	13.08
52	9.79	11.71	14.38
53	10.64	12.65	15.79
54	11.54	13.71	17.31
55	12.40	15.00	18.95
56	13.50	16.56	20.71
57	14.80	18.17	22.58
58	16.30	20.15	24.56
59	18.05	22.32	26.62
60	20.15	24.53	28.79

University Life

TABLE IV
Typical Deposit Term Plan

Issue Age	Premium Per $1,000	First-Year Deposit	Tenth-Year Refund*	Average Annual Cost Per $1,000
20	$ 2.64	$ 5.40	$14.00	$ 1.78
21	2.65	5.40	14.00	1.79
22	2.67	5.78	15.00	1.75
23	2.71	6.17	16.00	1.73
24	2.75	6.17	16.00	1.77
25	2.81	6.17	16.00	1.83
26	2.88	6.17	16.00	1.90
27	2.98	6.55	17.00	1.94
28	3.09	6.94	18.00	1.98
29	3.21	6.94	18.00	2.10
30	3.34	6.94	18.00	2.23
31	3.49	6.94	18.00	2.38
32	3.64	6.94	18.00	2.53
33	3.82	7.32	19.00	2.65
34	4.02	7.32	19.00	2.85
35	4.24	7.32	19.00	3.07
36	4.49	7.32	19.00	3.32
37	4.78	7.71	20.00	3.55
38	5.12	7.71	20.00	3.89
39	5.50	8.10	21.00	4.21
40	5.93	8.10	21.00	4.64
41	6.39	8.48	22.00	5.04
42	6.84	8.87	23.00	5.43
43	7.31	9.25	24.00	5.84
44	7.81	9.64	25.00	
45	8.20	9.64	25.00	6.66
46	8.57	10.02	26.00	6.97
47	9.05	10.41	27.00	7.39
48	9.67	10.79	28.00	7.95
49	10.41	11.18	29.00	8.63
50	11.30	11.57	30.00	9.46
51	12.33	11.95	31.00	10.43
52	13.51	12.34	32.00	11.54
53	14.84	12.72	33.00	12.81
54	16.34	13.11	34.00	14.25
55	18.00	13.49	35.00	15.85
56	19.83	14.26	37.00	17.56
57	21.84	15.03	39.00	19.44
58	24.04	15.42	40.00	21.58
59	26.42	16.19	42.00	23.84
60	29.00	16.96	44.00	26.30

* First-year deposit, compounded at 10% per year

158

OLD LINE LIFE

TABLE V

Typical Decreasing Term Plans (Annual Premiums/$1,000)

Issue Age	Dec. Term to Age 65	Dec. Term to Age 70	Dec. Term to Age 100
20	$ 2.46	$ 2.50	$ 4.60
21	2.52	2.57	4.77
22	2.58	2.64	4.93
23	2.65	2.73	5.14
24	2.72	2.82	5.34
25	2.79	2.92	5.55
26	2.87	3.02	5.78
27	2.96	3.13	6.01
28	3.05	3.25	6.26
29	3.15	3.37	6.52
30	3.25	3.50	6.80
31	3.37	3.65	7.11
32	3.49	3.80	7.44
33	3.62	3.96	7.79
34	3.76	4.13	8.16
35	3.92	4.33	8.55
36	4.08	4.52	8.96
37	4.26	4.74	9.40
38	4.45	4.97	9.81
39	4.65	5.21	10.36
40	4.86	5.47	10.90
41	5.08	5.77	11.50
42	5.31	6.11	12.12
43	5.56	6.51	12.78
44	5.82	6.96	13.48
45	6.15	7.46	14.21
46	6.52	7.98	15.00
47	6.92	8.52	15.84
48	7.29	9.11	16.73
49	7.68	9.73	17.69
50	8.18	10.39	18.70
51	8.65	11.13	19.80
52	9.22	12.01	21.00
53	9.85	12.99	22.28
54	10.59	14.08	23.63
55	11.30	15.26	25.09
56		16.56	26.63
57		17.96	28.30
58		19.50	30.07
59		22.02	31.95
60		24.96	34.00

OCCIDENTAL

TABLE VI

Typical Straight-Line Decreasing Term Plans with Level-off
Ending/Annual Premium/$1,000

Issue Age	15-Year Dec. Term	20-Year Dec. Term	25-Year Dec. Term	30-Year Dec. Term
20	$ 2.10	$ 2.12	$ 2.16	$2.24
21	2.11	2.13	2.17	2.26
22	2.12	2.14	2.18	2.28
23	2.13	2.15	2.20	2.30
24	2.14	2.16	2.22	2.32
25	2.15	2.17	2.24	2.34
26	2.16	2.18	2.26	2.37
27	2.17	2.19	2.29	2.41
28	2.18	2.20	2.32	2.46
29	2.19	2.21	2.35	2.53
30	2.20	2.22	2.39	2.61
31	2.24	2.30	2.51	2.75
32	2.28	2.40	2.66	2.92
33	2.35	2.52	2.82	3.12
34	2.45	2.66	3.02	3.35
35	2.58	2.83	3.25	3.61
36	2.75	3.05	3.51	3.90
37	2.95	3.29	3.81	4.23
38	3.18	3.57	4.16	4.62
39	3.46	3.88	4.54	5.07
40	3.78	4.22	4.97	5.57
41	4.12	4.60	5.51	6.12
42	4.48	5.02	6.10	6.72
43	4.87	5.48	6.70	7.39
44	5.27	5.99	7.33	8.11
45	5.70	6.54	7.98	8.90
46	6.22	7.14	8.65	
47	6.78	7.80	9.39	
48	7.39	8.52	10.19	
49	8.06	9.31	11.08	
50	8.78	10.17	12.04	
51	9.57	11.11		
52	10.42	12.13		
53	11.34	13.24		
54	12.33	14.46		
55	13.40	15.79		
56	14.55			
57	15.78			
58	17.10			
59	18.49			
60	19.96			

TABLE VII
Typical In-Between Decreasing Term Plans
(Annual Premiums/$1,000)

Issue Age	15 Years	20 Years	25 Years	30 Years
20	$ 1.60	$ 1.62	$ 1.63	$1.85
21	1.63	1.65	1.70	1.88
22	1.66	1.68	1.78	1.92
23	1.69	1.71	1.86	1.97
24	1.71	1.74	1.94	2.03
25	1.74	1.77	2.01	2.10
26	1.79	1.81	2.08	2.18
27	1.86	1.89	2.16	2.26
28	1.92	1.95	2.24	2.34
29	1.98	2.00	2.32	2.44
30	2.05	2.07	2.40	2.57
31	2.15	2.17	2.50	2.77
32	2.26	2.30	2.64	3.00
33	2.40	2.47	2.83	3.27
34	2.56	2.63	3.08	3.58
35	2.74	2.83	3.40	3.92
36	2.94	3.03	3.68	4.30
37	3.15	3.25	3.98	4.71
38	3.37	3.55	4.30	5.16
39	3.61	3.88	4.60	5.66
40	3.88	4.20	4.86	6.21
41	4.19	4.56	5.44	6.81
42	4.50	4.94	6.10	7.46
43	4.86	5.38	6.65	8.16
44	5.23	5.75	7.30	8.91
45	5.68	6.15	8.00	9.70
46	6.12	6.82	8.80	
47	6.60	7.67	9.52	
48	7.14	8.49	10.48	
49	7.69	9.38	11.40	
50	8.18	10.35	12.50	
51	9.08	11.29		
52	10.18	12.52		
53	11.37	13.67		
54	12.60	14.95		
55	13.82	16.60		
56	15.00			
57	16.30			
58	17.70			
59	19.22			
60	20.79			

GEORGIA INT'L

TABLE VIII
Typical 7½% Mortgage Term (Annual Premiums/$1,000)

Issue Age	15 Years	20 Years	25 Years	30 Years
20	$ 2.33	$ 2.39	$ 2.50	$ 2.67
21	2.36	2.43	2.55	2.75
22	2.41	2.48	2.61	2.83
23	2.45	2.54	2.68	2.93
24	2.50	2.60	2.76	3.04
25	2.56	2.67	2.85	3.16
26	2.62	2.75	2.95	3.29
27	2.68	2.82	3.05	3.42
28	2.73	2.89	3.14	3.55
29	2.79	2.97	3.25	3.69
30	2.86	3.06	3.37	3.85
31	2.94	3.17	3.52	4.04
32	3.04	3.31	3.70	4.28
33	3.17	3.48	3.91	4.57
34	3.33	3.68	4.18	4.92
35	3.53	3.93	4.49	5.35
36	3.75	4.20	4.83	5.82
37	3.97	4.48	5.19	6.32
38	4.21	4.78	5.56	6.86
39	4.46	5.11	5.96	7.44
40	4.75	5.47	6.41	8.07
41	5.07	5.87	6.91	8.78
42	5.44	6.33	7.48	9.56
43	5.87	6.85	8.13	10.43
44	6.35	7.44	8.86	11.41
45	6.90	8.12	9.70	12.49
46	7.49	8.84	10.58	
47	8.11	9.60	11.54	
48	8.76	10.41	12.57	
49	9.45	11.28	13.68	
50	10.21	12.22	14.87	
51	11.03	13.24		
52	11.94	14.35		
53	12.95	15.56		
54	14.06	16.88		
55	15.30	18.31		
56	16.63			
57	18.06			
58	19.59			
59	21.21			
60	22.93			

TABLE IX
Comparison of 15-Year Decreasing Term Plans
(Rate of Decrease)

Start of Year	Straight-Line Term	In-Between Term	7½% Mortgage Term
1	$1,000	$1,000	$1,000
2	933	946	963
3	867	891	923
4	800	834	879
5	733	775	832
6	667	715	781
7	600	652	727
8	533	588	668
9	467	522	605
10	400	454	537
11	333	384	463
12	267	312	384
13	200	237	299
14	200	161	200
15	200	82	200

A fifteen-year straight-line decreasing term plan without the level-off feature would reduce as follows:

14	133
15	67

TABLE X
Comparison of 20-Year Decreasing Term Plans
(Rate of Decrease)

Start of Year	Straight-Line Term	In-Between Term	7½% Mortgage Term
1	$1,000	$1,000	$1,000
2	950	963	978
3	900	925	954
4	850	885	928
5	800	844	900
6	750	802	870
7	700	759	837
8	650	715	802
9	600	669	764
10	550	621	723
11	500	574	679
12	450	523	632
13	400	472	581
14	350	419	526
15	300	364	466
16	250	308	403
17	200	250	334
18	200	190	259
19	200	129	200
20	200	66	200

A twenty-year straight-line decreasing term plan without the level-off feature would reduce as follows:

18	150
19	100
20	50

TABLE XI

Comparison of 25-Year Decreasing Term Plans
(Rate of Decrease)

Start of Year	Straight-Line Term	In-Between Term	7½% Mortgage Term
1	$1,000	$1,000	$1,000
2	960	973	986
3	920	944	971
4	880	915	955
5	840	885	937
6	800	855	918
7	760	823	897
8	720	790	875
9	680	756	851
10	640	721	825
11	600	685	798
12	560	649	768
13	520	611	736
14	480	572	701
15	440	531	663
16	400	490	623
17	360	447	580
18	320	403	533
19	280	358	482
20	240	311	428
21	200	263	369
22	200	214	306
23	200	162	238
24	200	110	200
25	200	56	200

A twenty-five-year straight-line decreasing term plan without the level-off feature would reduce as follows:

22	160
23	120
24	80
25	40

TABLE XII
Comparison of 30-Year Decreasing Term Plans
(Rate of Decrease)

Start of Year	Straight-Line Term	In-Between Term	7½% Mortgage Term
1	$1,000	$1,000	$1,000
2	967	979	991
3	933	957	981
4	900	935	971
5	867	912	959
6	833	888	947
7	800	864	933
8	767	839	919
9	733	813	903
10	700	786	887
11	667	759	868
12	633	731	849
13	600	702	828
14	567	672	805
15	533	641	781
16	500	609	755
17	467	576	726
18	433	542	696
19	400	508	663
20	367	472	628
21	333	435	590
22	300	397	548
23	267	358	504
24	233	318	456
25	200	276	405
26	200	234	349
27	200	190	290
28	200	144	225
29	200	98	200
30	200	50	200

A thirty-year straight-line decreasing term plan without the level-off feature would reduce as follows:

26	167
27	133
28	100
29	67
30	33

COMMISSIONERS 1958 STANDARD
ORDINARY MORTALITY TABLE

Age	Number Living	Number of Deaths	Deaths Per 1,000	Expectation of Life
0	10,000,000	70,800	7.08	68.30
1	9,929,200	17,475	1.76	67.78
2	9,911,725	15,066	1.52	66.90
3	9,896,659	14,449	1.46	66.00
4	9,882,210	13,835	1.40	65.10
5	9,868,375	13,322	1.35	64.19
6	9,855,053	12,812	1.30	63.27
7	9,842,241	12,401	1.26	62.35
8	9,829,840	12,091	1.23	61.43
9	9,817,749	11,879	1.21	60.51
10	9,805,870	11,865	1.21	59.58
11	9,794,005	12,047	1.23	58.65
12	9,781,958	12,325	1.26	57.72
13	9,769,633	12,896	1.32	56.80
14	9,756,737	13,562	1.39	55.87
15	9,743,175	14,225	1.46	54.95
16	9,728,950	14,983	1.54	54.03
17	9,713,967	15,737	1.62	53.11
18	9,698,230	16,390	1.69	52.19
19	9,681,840	16,846	1.74	51.28
20	9,664,994	17,300	1.79	50.37
21	9,647,694	17,655	1.83	49.46
22	9,630,039	17,912	1.86	48.55
23	9,612,127	18,167	1.89	47.64
24	9,593,960	18,324	1.91	46.73
25	9,575,636	18,481	1.93	45.82
26	9,557,155	18,732	1.96	44.90
27	9,538,423	18,981	1.99	43.99
28	9,519,442	19,324	2.03	43.08
29	9,500,118	19,760	2.08	42.16
30	9,480,358	20,193	2.13	41.25
31	9,460,165	20,718	2.19	40.34
32	9,439,447	21,239	2.25	39.43
33	9,418,208	21,850	2.32	38.51
34	9,396,358	22,551	2.40	37.60
35	9,373,807	23,528	2.51	36.69
36	9,350,279	24,685	2.64	35.78
37	9,325,594	26,112	2.80	34.88
38	9,299,482	27,991	3.01	33.97
39	9,271,491	30,132	3.25	33.07
40	9,241,359	32,622	3.53	32.18
41	9,208,737	35,362	3.84	31.29
42	9,173,375	38,253	4.17	30.41
43	9,135,122	41,382	4.53	29.54
44	9,093,740	44,741	4.92	28.67
45	9,048,999	48,412	5.35	27.81
46	9,000,587	52,473	5.83	26.95
47	8,948,114	56,910	6.36	26.11
48	8,891,204	61,794	6.95	25.27
49	8,829,410	67,104	7.60	24.45

COMMISSIONERS 1958 STANDARD
ORDINARY MORTALITY TABLE

Age	Number Living	Number of Deaths	Deaths Per 1,000	Expectation of Life
50	8,762,306	72,902	8.32	23.63
51	8,689,404	79,160	9.11	22.82
52	8,610,244	85,758	9.96	22.03
53	8,524,486	92,832	10.89	21.25
54	8,431,654	100,337	11.90	20.47
55	8,331,317	108,307	13.00	19.71
56	8,223,010	116,849	14.21	18.97
57	8,106,161	125,970	15.54	18.23
58	7,980,191	135,663	17.00	17.51
59	7,844,528	145,830	18.59	16.81
60	7,698,698	156,592	20.34	16.12
61	7,542,106	167,736	22.24	15.44
62	7,374,370	179,271	24.31	14.78
63	7,195,099	191,174	26.57	14.14
64	7,003,925	203,394	29.04	13.51
65	6,800,531	215,917	31.75	12.90
66	6,584,614	228,749	34.74	12.31
67	6,355,865	241,777	38.04	11.73
68	6,114,088	254,835	41.68	11.17
69	5,859,253	267,241	45.61	10.64
70	5,592,012	278,426	49.79	10.12
71	5,313,586	278,731	54.15	9.63
72	5,025,855	294,766	58.65	9.15
73	4,731,089	299,289	63.26	8.69
74	4,431,800	301,894	68.12	8.24
75	4,129,906	303,011	73.37	7.81
76	3,826,895	303,014	79.18	7.39
77	3,523,881	301,997	85.70	6.98
78	3,221,884	299,829	93.06	6.59
79	2,922,055	295,683	101.19	6.21
80	2,626,372	288,848	109.98	5.85
81	2,337,524	278,983	119.35	5.51
82	2,058,541	265,902	129.17	5.19
83	1,792,639	249,858	139.38	4.89
84	1,542,781	231,433	150.01	4.60
85	1,311,348	211,311	161.14	4.32
86	1,100,037	190,108	172.82	4.06
87	909,929	168.455	185.13	3.80
88	741,474	146,997	198.25	3.55
89	594,477	126,303	212.46	3.31
90	468,174	106,809	228.14	3.06
91	361,365	88,813	245.77	2.82
92	272,552	72,480	265.93	2.58
93	200,072	57,881	289.30	2.33
94	142,191	45,026	316.66	2.07
95	97,165	34,128	351.24	1.80
96	63,037	25,250	400.56	1.51
97	37,787	18,456	488.42	1.18
98	19,331	12,916	668.15	.83
99	6,415	6,415	1000.00	.50

COMPOUND INTEREST TABLES
Accumulation of One Dollar Deposited at the Beginning of Each Year

Years	3.5%	4%	4.5%	5%	6%
1	1.0350	1.0400	1.0450	1.0500	1.0600
2	2.1062	2.1216	2.1370	2.1525	2.1836
3	3.2149	3.2465	3.2782	3.3101	3.3746
4	4.3625	4.4163	4.4707	4.5256	4.6371
5	5.5502	5.6330	5.7169	5.8019	5.9753
6	6.7794	6.8983	7.0192	7.1420	7.3938
7	8.0517	8.2142	8.3800	8.5491	8.8975
8	9.3685	9.5828	9.8021	10.0266	10.4913
9	10.7314	11.0061	11.2882	11.5779	12.1808
10	12.1420	12.4864	12.8412	13.2068	13.9716
11	13.6020	14.0258	14.4640	14.9171	15.8699
12	15.1130	15.6268	16.1599	16.7130	17.8821
13	16.6770	17.2919	17.9321	18.5986	20.0151
14	18.2957	19.0236	19.7841	20.5786	22.2760
15	19.9710	20.8245	21.7193	22.6575	24.6725
16	21.7050	22.6975	23.7417	24.8404	27.2129
17	23.4997	24.6454	25.8551	27.1324	29.9057
18	25.3572	26.6712	28.0636	29.5390	32.7600
19	27.2797	28.7781	30.3714	32.0660	35.7856
20	29.2695	30.9692	32.7831	34.7193	38.9927
21	31.3289	33.2480	35.3034	37.5052	42.3923
22	33.4604	35.6179	37.9370	40.4305	45.9958
23	35.6665	38.0826	40.6892	43.5020	49.8156
24	37.9499	40.6459	43.5652	46.7271	53.8645
25	40.3131	43.3117	46.5706	50.1135	58.1564
26	42.7591	46.0842	49.7113	53.6691	62.7058
27	45.2906	48.9676	52.9933	57.4026	67.5281
28	47.9108	51.9663	56.4230	61.3227	72.6398
29	50.6227	55.0849	60.0071	65.4388	78.0582
30	53.4295	58.3283	63.7524	69.7608	83.8017
31	56.3345	61.7015	67.6662	74.2988	89.8898
32	59.3412	65.2095	71.7562	79.0638	96.3432
33	62.4532	68.8579	76.0303	84.0670	103.1838
34	65.6740	72.6522	80.4966	89.3203	110.4348
35	69.0076	76.5983	85.1640	94.8363	118.1209
36	72.4579	80.7022	90.0413	100.6281	126.2681
37	76.0289	84.9703	95.1382	106.7095	134.9042
38	79.7249	89.4091	100.4644	113.0950	144.0585
39	83.5503	94.0255	106.0303	119.7998	153.7620
40	87.5095	98.8265	111.8467	126.8398	164.0477

COMPOUND INTEREST TABLES
Accumulation of One Dollar Deposited at the Beginning of Each Year

Years	8%	10%	12%	15%
1	1.0800	1.1000	1.1200	1.1500
2	2.2464	2.3100	2.3744	2.4725
3	3.5061	3.6410	3.7793	3.9934
4	4.8666	5.1051	5.3528	5.7424
5	6.3359	6.7156	7.1152	7.7537
6	7.9228	8.4872	9.0890	10.0668
7	9.6366	10.4359	11.2997	12.7268
8	11.4876	12.5795	13.7757	15.7858
9	13.4866	14.9374	16.5487	19.3037
10	15.6455	17.5312	19.6546	23.3493
11	17.9771	20.3843	23.1331	28.0017
12	20.4953	23.5227	27.0291	33.3519
13	23.2149	26.9750	31.3926	39.5047
14	26.1521	30.7725	36.2797	46.5804
15	29.3243	34.9497	41.7533	54.7175
16	32.7502	39.5447	47.8837	64.0751
17	36.4502	44.5992	54.7497	74.8364
18	40.4463	50.1591	62.4397	87.2118
19	44.7620	56.2750	71.0524	101.4436
20	49.4229	63.0025	80.6987	117.8101
21	54.4568	70.4027	91.5026	136.6316
22	59.8933	78.5430	103.6029	158.2764
23	65.7648	87.4973	117.1552	183.1678
24	72.1059	97.3471	132.3339	211.7930
25	78.9544	108.1818	149.3339	244.7120
26	86.3508	120.0999	168.3740	282.5688
27	94.3388	133.2099	189.6989	326.1041
28	102.9659	147.6309	213.5828	376.1697
29	112.2832	163.4940	240.3327	433.7451
30	122.3459	180.9434	270.2926	499.9569
31	133.2135	200.1378	303.8477	576.1005
32	144.9506	221.2515	341.4294	663.6655
33	157.6267	244.4767	383.5210	764.3654
34	171.3168	270.0244	430.6635	880.1702
35	186.1021	298.1268	483.4631	1013.3757
36	202.0703	329.0395	542.5987	1166.4975
37	219.3159	363.0434	608.8305	1342.6222
38	237.9412	400.4478	683.0102	1545.1655
39	258.0565	441.5926	766.0914	1778.0903
40	279.7810	486.8518	859.1424	2045.9539

COMPOUND INTEREST TABLES
Accumulation of One Dollar Principal

Years	3.5%	4%	4.5%	5%	6%
1	1.0350	1.0400	1.0450	1.0500	1.0600
2	1.0712	1.0816	1.0920	1.1025	1.1236
3	1.1087	1.1249	1.1412	1.1576	1.1910
4	1.1475	1.1699	1.1925	1.2155	1.2625
5	1.1877	1.2167	1.2462	1.2763	1.3382
6	1.2293	1.2653	1.3023	1.3401	1.4185
7	1.2723	1.3159	1.3609	1.4071	1.5036
8	1.3168	1.3686	1.4221	1.4775	1.5938
9	1.3629	1.4233	1.4861	1.5513	1.6895
10	1.4106	1.4802	1.5530	1.6289	1.7908
11	1.4600	1.5395	1.6229	1.7103	1.8983
12	1.5111	1.6010	1.6959	1.7959	2.0122
13	1.5640	1.6651	1.7722	1.8856	2.1329
14	1.6187	1.7317	1.8519	1.9799	2.2609
15	1.6753	1.8009	1.9353	2.0789	2.3966
16	1.7340	1.8730	2.0224	2.1829	2.5404
17	1.7947	1.9479	2.1134	2.2920	2.6928
18	1.8575	2.0258	2.2085	2.4066	2.8543
19	1.9225	2.1068	2.3079	2.5270	3.0256
20	1.9898	2.1911	2.4117	2.6533	3.2071
21	2.0594	2.2788	2.5202	2.7860	3.3996
22	2.1315	2.3699	2.6337	2.9253	3.6035
23	2.2061	2.4647	2.7522	3.0715	3.8197
24	2.2833	2.5633	2.8760	3.2251	4.0489
25	2.3632	2.6658	3.0054	3.3864	4.2919
26	2.4460	2.7725	3.1407	3.5557	4.5494
27	2.5316	2.8834	3.2820	3.7335	4.8223
28	2.6202	2.9987	3.4297	3.9201	5.1117
29	2.7119	3.1187	3.5840	4.1161	5.4184
30	2.8068	3.2434	3.7453	4.3219	5.7435
31	2.9050	3.3731	3.9139	4.5380	6.0881
32	3.0067	3.5081	4.0900	4.7649	6.4534
33	3.1119	3.6484	4.2740	5.0032	6.8406
34	3.2209	3.7943	4.4664	5.2533	7.2510
35	3.3336	3.9461	4.6673	5.5160	7.6861
36	3.4503	4.1039	4.8774	5.7918	8.1473
37	3.5710	4.2681	5.0969	6.0814	8.6361
38	3.6960	4.4388	5.3263	6.3855	9.1543
39	3.8254	4.6164	5.5659	6.7048	9.7035
40	3.9593	4.8010	5.8164	7.0400	10.2857

COMPOUND INTEREST TABLES
Accumulation of One Dollar Principal

Years	8%	10%	12%	15%
1	1.0800	1.1000	1.1200	1.1500
2	1.1664	1.2100	1.2544	1.3225
3	1.2597	1.3310	1.4049	1.5209
4	1.3605	1.4641	1.5735	1.7490
5	1.4693	1.6105	1.7623	2.0114
6	1.5869	1.7716	1.9738	2.3131
7	1.7138	1.9487	2.2107	2.6600
8	1.8509	2.1436	2.4760	3.0590
9	1.9990	2.3579	2.7731	3.5179
10	2.1589	2.5937	3.1058	4.0456
11	2.3316	2.8531	3.4785	4.6524
12	2.5182	3.1384	3.8960	5.3503
13	2.7196	3.4523	4.3635	6.1528
14	2.9372	3.7975	4.8871	7.0757
15	3.1722	4.1772	5.4736	8.1371
16	3.4259	4.5950	6.1304	9.3576
17	3.7000	5.0545	6.8660	10.7613
18	3.9960	5.5599	7.6900	12.3755
19	4.3157	6.1159	8.6128	14.2318
20	4.6610	6.7275	9.6463	16.3665
21	5.0338	7.4002	10.8038	18.8215
22	5.4365	8.1403	12.1003	21.6447
23	5.8715	8.9543	13.5523	24.8915
24	6.3412	9.8497	15.1786	28.6252
25	6.8485	10.8347	17.0001	32.9190
26	7.3964	11.9182	19.0401	37.8568
27	7.9881	13.1100	21.3249	43.5353
28	8.6271	14.4210	23.8839	50.0656
29	9.3173	15.8631	26.7499	57.5755
30	10.0627	17.4494	29.9599	66.2118
31	10.8677	19.1943	33.5551	76.1435
32	11.7371	21.1138	37.5817	87.5651
33	12.6760	23.2252	42.0915	100.6998
34	13.6901	25.5477	47.1425	115.8048
35	14.7853	28.1024	52.7996	133.1755
36	15.9682	30.9127	59.1356	153.1519
37	17.2456	34.0039	66.2318	176.1246
38	18.6253	37.4043	74.1797	202.5433
39	20.1153	41.1448	83.0812	232.9248
40	21.7245	45.2593	93.0510	267.8635

INDEX